FISHING
LAKE SUPERIOR

A complete guide to stream,
shoreline, and open-water angling

FISHING
LAKE SUPERIOR

A complete guide to stream,
shoreline, and open-water angling

SHAWN PERICH

Illustrations by Jeff Sonstegard

University of Minnesota Press

Minneapolis / London

Fish species illustrations are from <u>Fish of Lake Superior</u>, a publication of the University of Wisconsin Sea Grant College Program, and are used with permission.

Canadian safety regulations are reprinted with permission from <u>Safe Boating Guide</u>, a publication of the Canadian Government Publishing Centre.

Published by the University of Minnesota Press
111 Third Avenue South, Suite 290
Minneapolis, MN 55401-2520
http://www.upress.umn.edu

A Cataloging-in-Publication record for this book is available from the Library of Congress.

ISBN 0-8166-4200-1 (PB)

Printed in the United States of America on acid-free paper

The University of Minnesota is an equal-opportunity educator and employer.

13 12 11 10 09 08 07 06   10 9 8 7 6 5 4 3 2

To my dad, Dan Perich:

If I fish too much, it's your fault.

Contents

Lake Superior

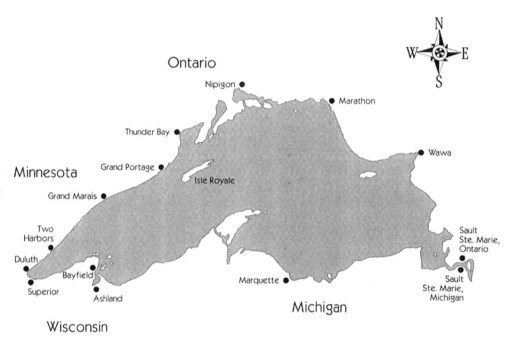

Ontario

Nipigon •

• Marathon

Thunder Bay •

Minnesota

Grand Portage •

• Wawa

Isle Royale

Grand Marais •

Two
Harbors •

Duluth •

Sault
Ste. Marie,
Ontario

Bayfield •

Marquette •

Superior •

Ashland •

Sault
Ste. Marie,
Michigan

Michigan

Wisconsin

Introduction

I REMEMBER A SUNNY April day when my father picked me up from kindergarten at noon. On his way home from steelhead fishing, he'd discovered that spawning smelt were running literally bank to bank in Duluth's Lester River, so we went to dip-net a pailful. At that time, the mid-sixties, vast schools of smelt—and few other fish—swam in western Lake Superior. I can still see the black schools of smelt holding in the Lester's clear currents, and remember running along the bank to scoop up extra-large smelt with my hands. Then my father picked me up and waded out to deeper water, where I scooped up so many smelt I could hardly hold the dip net. So began my Lake Superior fishing career.

Rainbow Smelt

Growing up in Duluth, I explored steelhead streams, skipped school to fish for St. Louis River walleyes, and even cast for northern pike off the Duluth Ship Canal piers. The lake was different then, ravaged by environmental carelessness. Sport-fishing boats were an uncommon sight.

I remember trolling for coho salmon in the early '70s, when they first returned to the French River, and later fishing for them through the ice in the Sucker River. That year marked the beginning of an exciting new era for Lake Superior, when sea lamprey control coupled with stocking of lake trout and Pacific salmon created a superb sport fishery. Unfortunately for me, I moved away from the lake just as this new fishery blossomed, although weekends and vacations always brought me back. Finally, I moved to Grand Marais, Minnesota, in 1987. Since then I've spent a lot of time on a boat or in waders.

Sea lamprey control, coupled with stocking of lake trout and Pacific Salmon, created a superb sport fishery.

I make no claims to be an expert Lake Superior fisherman. However, I am a journalist as well as a fisherman, so I know how to ask questions and take notes. A number of persons took time from their day to answer those questions and share their expertise. Talking to people around the lake, I discovered some areas of common ground. First, although the more glamorous silver fish such as salmon and steelhead may attract anglers to Lake Superior, the underrated lake trout support the fishery. Second, although the lake's devastated fisheries have enjoyed a dramatic comeback, the future remains precarious. Greedy individuals—with nets and fishing rods—can destroy it again through overfishing. Sea lamprey have not disappeared, and experience tells us that other ecological disasters might be lurking around the corner. It will take great effort to conserve and protect this spectacular resource.

You'll notice the book doesn't include fish-stocking information, seasons and bag limits, or brand names of tackle and equipment. That sort of information can change from year to year. Disease in a fish hatchery can wipe out annual stockings. And as I researched around the lake, it became apparent that favorite lures change with locales. A hot spoon in Wawa may be unavailable in Ashland—and it might not catch fish even if it were available. Whenever you plan to fish a new area on the lake, find out what the locals use and how they fish before heading out. Also ask about potentially dangerous conditions. Weather on Lake Superior can change rapidly. Safety, not catching fish, should always be your priority. This book is not the last word on fishing Lake Superior. It is merely a guide intended to show you necessary fishing techniques and help you find places to fish. After that, you're on your own. Fishing isn't rocket science, but experience is the best teacher. Go fish.

Lake Trout

Acknowledgments

THE FOLLOWING PERSONS generously provided their expertise to this book.

Ralph Brzezinski, charter captain, Bayfield, Wisconsin; Rich Brummer, charter captain, Grand Portage, Minnesota; Bill Deephouse, Michigan DNR; Gord Ellis, outdoor writer, Thunder Bay, Ontario; Deb Ethier, Boat and Water Safety, Minnesota DNR; Wayne Fairchild, marine mechanics instructor, Duluth, Minnesota; Jeff Gunderson, Minnesota Sea Grant, Duluth, Minnesota; Ray Juttenen, Michigan DNR; Gary and Barb Hansen, Fisherman's Cove, Port Wing, Wisconsin; Chuck Hutterli, charter captain, Rossport, Ontario; Roger and Carolyn LaPenter, Anglers All, Ashland, Wisconsin; Jim Keuten, tackle store owner, Duluth, Minnesota; Lee Newman, United States Fish and Wildlife Service, Ashland, Wisconsin; Dick Lenski, angler, Grand Marais, Minnesota; Dan Parkinson, angler, Superior, Wisconsin; Dave Raikko, charter captain, Marquette, Michigan; Don Schreiner, Minnesota DNR; Steve Scott, Michigan DNR; James Smedley, outdoor writer, Wawa, Ontario.

Changes In the "Big Pond"

THE OLD LAKE TROUT heard the click of the cannonball bouncing along the bottom long before she saw the flash of the dodger, a spark of light in the murky depths. Deliberately, the laker turned toward the flash, rapidly closing the distance with a few strokes of her powerful tail. She smelled the powerful lure of fish-attracting scent and saw the small plastic squid undulating behind the flasher. She swam toward the squid and then abruptly turned away. Perhaps the three herring she'd captured that morning had sated her appetite, or maybe during her four decades in the lake she'd learned to avoid human baits and nets.

The lake had changed during the ancient redfin's life. But fish, the scientists say, cannot comprehend. The old lake trout was unaware that overfishing, the sea lamprey, and pollution had wiped out the native lake trout in every Great Lake but Superior. And she didn't know that on Superior, populations of native brook trout, whitefish, chubs, sturgeon, and other species were decimated. Nor did she know that the silvery smelt that she occasionally ate were invaders, like the sea lamprey; while the sea lampreys killed trout and other fish, the prolific smelt wreaked havoc with the native herring population.

Overfishing, the sea lamprey, and pollution wiped out the native lake trout in every Great Lake but Superior.

She certainly didn't know that the lake trout who in later years became her neighbors were spawned in a government fish hatchery. She was one of the last of her strain, a population of lake trout that had spawned on an offshore shoal every autumn for centuries. When this particular trout was born, the lake trout that spawned on that shoal were already in trouble. Just twenty years earlier, commercial netters had discovered the shoal and learned that the trout spawned there every year in the first week of October. Each autumn, prime redfin lake trout filled dozens of fish boxes. When the old lake trout was born, netters were already complaining that fishing wasn't what it used to be. Some of the lake trout they caught had round, ugly scars on their sides—calling card of the predatory sea lamprey, which left a path of destruction as it made its way through the Great Lakes via the St. Lawrence Seaway.

Within a few years, the shoal's lake trout were nearly gone. The autumn that this old lake trout grew large enough to get tangled in the mesh of a gill net was the year that the netters gave up. So, she was a survivor. She and a handful of other lake trout roamed the shoal, feeding on herring, which also dwindled in numbers. Somehow, enough trout avoided the lampreys so that a few spawned every autumn during the first week of October. But during the span of the old lake trout's life, Lake Superior had changed forever.

If you tell John Olson that somewhere in Lake Superior swims a lake trout the same age as he, he'll laugh and ask if the fish is bald, too. During the week, John is a carpenter, and he's helped build many of the vacation homes that now occupy the once-wild shores of Lake Superior. However, if John had his druthers, he'd go fishing every day. A trim cruiser rests on a trailer in his driveway,

During the span of the old lake trout's life, Lake Superior had changed forever.

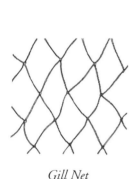

Gill Net

waiting for the weekend. John has fished Lake Superior since childhood. When he was a kid, his father took him fishing for steelhead as they made their spring spawning run up tributary streams. Sometimes they caught fish with sea lamprey still dangling from their sides. Later in the spring, they would dip-net bucketfuls of spawning smelt from the same streams. Sometimes they'd troll on the lake during the summer, but they rarely caught anything.

However, John can well remember when the trolling started to improve. First, the government began using a lamprey-specific poison to kill sea lampreys in the streams where they spawned. This action was coupled with massive fish stocking efforts, not only for lake trout, but also for species such as coho and chinook salmon. Although John was among the first in his town to get serious about trolling on Superior, it had taken him and other anglers several years to learn the secrets of catching fish on, as they called it, "the Big Pond."

During the 1970s and early 1980s, John's fishing success improved as trout and salmon numbers increased and as he learned effective ways to catch them. In fact, he still talks about the summer mornings when he trolled through huge schools of surface-feeding cohos. A typical catch during those years contained a silvery mix of cohos, steelhead, and chinooks, as well as the inevitable lake trout. Usually John fished within a mile of shore, where predator fish fed on large schools of smelt.

But John will tell you that during the late 1980s and early 1990s, the lake changed again. Smelt, an important nearshore forage fish, dwindled to the point that the spring dip-netting ritual no longer generated much excitement in Lake Superior communities. John still caught some cohos and chinooks, but in fewer numbers.

A typical catch during the 1970s and early 1980s might contain a silvery mix of cohos, steelhead, and chinooks, as well as the inevitable lake trout.

Today he releases all his wild steelhead to protect the population. The lake trout are still out there, but even they seem to be changing their habits. John's friend, a commercial netter, tells him lake herring have so increased in numbers that some of his catches rival the good old days. Both he and John wonder if lake trout are adapting to this off-shore food source. In fact, John has started venturing miles from shore to search for fish. Anglers like him can always find a new frontier.

Maybe someday he'll troll a bait past that old lake trout, and she'll make a mistake. The battle will be memorable, but the trout won't wind up in a cooler. John knows such fish are both relics left to remind us of what we have lost on Lake Superior and our hope for the future. The old trout will be released to return to her shoal. Perhaps someday, decades in the future, John's now ten-year-old son will catch one of her offspring.

Lake Trout

The Fish of Lake Superior

FROM PACIFIC SALMON TO NATIVE WALLEYES, Lake Superior supports a diverse sport-fish population. Most species are indigenous to the lake, but many others were introduced over the last century. While anglers welcome the steelhead and other game fish to the lake, some exotic species—such as the deadly sea lamprey—are upsetting Lake Superior's ecosystem.

Lake Trout

Lake trout are the most common game fish in Lake Superior, available to everyone from shore-casters to offshore trollers. A native species that supported commercial, subsistence, and sport fisheries from pre-Columbian times until the 1940s, the lake trout was nearly extirpated from Lake Superior through overfishing and predation by invading sea lampreys. Today the only naturally spawning populations in the Great Lakes occur in Lake Superior, where an estimated seventy-five percent of the lake trout are wild-bred. The fact that lakers are again numerous and beginning to thrive in Superior is a triumph of fisheries management.

However, the lake trout restoration effort of federal, state, provincial, and tribal fisheries agencies was neither easy nor quick. It has taken

Lake Trout

Today the only naturally spawning populations of lake trout in the Great Lakes occur in Lake Superior.

Today the only places where anglers can experience fishing as it was a century ago are remote offshore areas such as Michigan's Stannard Rock and Isle Royale.

thirty years to rebuild Superior's wild lake trout population to current levels; and hundreds of thousands of hatchery-raised lakers, all marked with clipped fins for identification, are still stocked each year. Despite today's more enlightened attitudes toward fish conservation, serious threats to the fishery still exist. Although the United States and Canada have instituted extensive sea lamprey control programs, this parasitic ocean fish has not yet been eradicated from the Great Lakes. Biologists estimate that the annual loss of lake trout to eel-like lampreys is equal to the total sport and commercial harvests on Lake Superior. In some portions of the lake, overharvest by netters and sport anglers has also depressed lake trout populations. To protect lake trout stocks, Wisconsin has established refuge areas where no netting or sport fishing is allowed.

Originally, Lake Superior contained numerous strains of lake trout, which spawned at different times and lived at various depths. Some grew to enormous sizes, with twenty- to forty-pounders common catches for old-time sport anglers. However, those large old trout—in Superior's cold waters a laker may live for forty years or more—were the most vulnerable to sea lampreys. Today the only places where anglers can experience fishing as it was a century ago are remote offshore areas such as Michigan's Stannard Rock and Isle Royale. Biologists believe these lake trout populations survived the lamprey onslaught because the parasites concentrated in nearshore waters. Nevertheless, these fish populations now face another onslaught, particularly at Isle Royale. Sport-fishing pressure has increased, and some unthinking "sports" fill their coolers with giant lakers. Many anglers, however, realize the value of these giant fish and practice catch-and-release.

Such attitudes must become the norm if we want these relic populations to flourish.

Today, even though many original strains are extinct, anglers can still notice differences among the lake trout they catch. An average catch of lake trout shows variations in the markings, coloration, and body shape of the fish, as well as in the edible qualities of the flesh. Lake trout fillets can vary from a deep salmon red color to pale yellow or white. Generally red and orange fillets are least oily and taste best, but pale filets are tasty, too. The fish most people prefer to catch are called redfins: lean, wild lakers with firm, red flesh.

Are They Safe To Eat?

Although by far the cleanest Great Lake, even wild Lake Superior has suffered from pollution. Some of the fish that swim in it are contaminated with chemicals that entered the lake through industrial and municipal wastes and polluted precipitation. You should study the health advisories for the area you plan to fish and follow the suggested guidelines for the amount of fish you should eat. Those most at risk from fish contaminants are young children, pregnant women, and women of childbearing age.

Remember, the guidelines need not deprive you of a fish dinner. Generally speaking, most smaller fish in Lake Superior are safe to eat. Those with the highest levels of contamination are usually large, fatty fish such as big lake trout, siscowets, or carp, none of which are very delectable, anyway.

Smaller lake trout, salmon, whitefish, walleyes, and other species can be safely eaten, especially if you take steps to reduce your risk. Keep smaller fish for eating, because younger fish have less time to accumulate contaminants. Fish species such as yellow perch and crappie are less likely to be contaminated. Remove the fat and skin from lake trout and other salmonids when you clean them. Be sure to trim the dark areas along the lateral line, which will improve the flavor, too. However, such trimming will not reduce mercury levels because mercury accumulates in muscle tissue.

Siscowets, an uncommon sport catch in most areas because they usually occupy very deep water, have a high fat content. Although nutritionists say that siscowets are high in healthy omega–3 oils, most anglers consider them virtually inedible.

Whether or not lake trout taste good quite often depends on the way they are cooked. Experiment with various recipes to find ones that you like best.

Brook Trout

Brook Trout

Nearly extinct from overfishing and industrialization, it is unlikely these once-prized fish will stage a comeback anytime soon.

During the nineteenth century, Lake Superior was *the* place to catch brook trout. Called coasters, these giant brook trout occupied nearshore waters of the lake and tributary streams. Although Ontario's Nipigon River and Wisconsin's Brule River were probably early sport angler's most popular destinations, they caught coasters in the vicinity of virtually every trout stream flowing into the lake. Early sport-fishing accounts tell of catching two- to four-pound brook trout by the basketful. The world record, a 14.8-pound monster, was caught in the Nipigon by Dr. J. W. Cook in 1916.

Today, coaster brook trout are nearly gone. Overfishing, logging, dams, industrial pollution, and competition with introduced trout and salmon species have reduced a once-abundant native fish to near extinction. Remnant populations exist in the Nipigon area and at Isle Royale. Michigan, Wisconsin, and Minnesota have all tried stocking brook trout, with little apparent success, although the odd brookie may show up anywhere—particularly near breakwalls and harbors or in tributary streams during the fall.

However, hope for the coasters' return lies in new restoration efforts being undertaken by some fish managers around the lake. Ontario has begun efforts to control water fluctations caused by dams on the Nipigon River, because low water levels in winter and spring expose newly hatched brook trout on the spawning beds. Restrictive bag limits protect the Nipigon brook trout from over-harvest. Elsewhere, the United States Fish and Wildlife Service is working with tribal fish managers in an attempt to reestablish spawning populations of brook trout in suitable habitat. State fish managers are dragging their feet regarding brook trout restoration efforts, primarily due to their past lack of success. Although current efforts by Ontario and the tribes should save the coaster from extinction, it is unlikely these once-prized fish will stage a comeback anytime soon.

Rainbow Trout

Rainbow trout, or steelhead, were first stocked in Lake Superior during the 1880s, and they quickly adapted to their new home. Spring spawners, they ascend tributaries ranging from tiny creeks to wide rivers shortly after ice-out. Young rainbows spend the first two or three years of their lives in the stream, growing to a length of seven or eight inches. Then they "smolt," migrating downstream to the big lake, where they spend one to three years feeding before returning to the stream to spawn. Unlike Pacific salmon, they do not die after spawning, but instead return to the lake. In fact, they may spawn two or three times.

During the 1960s and 1970s, when the native lake trout population bottomed out and Pacific salmon had not yet become established, steelhead were the primary sport fish sought by Lake Superior anglers. But in recent years, anglers and fisheries managers have become concerned that steelhead populations have declined. No one is certain why, but overharvest by anglers, competition from growing numbers of other trout and

Rainbow Trout

Also known as steelhead, the rainbow trout was introduced to Lake Superior in the latter part of the nineteenth century.

salmon, and, in some areas, netting are likely culprits. Minnesota and Wisconsin adopted restrictive trophy-only bag limits in an effort to boost numbers of wild fish. Although rainbow trout are stocked in Lake Superior, most fisheries managers believe that with proper protection wild steelhead populations can be sustained through natural reproduction.

Nevertheless, stocking of domesticated strains such as the Kamloops rainbow and Skamania steelhead will likely continue. Both strains are considered easier to catch than the wild steelhead, which roam throughout the vast lake. Kamloops rainbows, stocked by Minnesota, stage near river

What is it? Indentifying Superior's Salmonids

In the landing net flops a large fish so brightly chromed that it has few spots or other markings. Novice and even experienced anglers might well ask, "What is it?" On Lake Superior, knowing what you've caught is important, because some species, such as rainbow trout, may have size limits or other bag limit restrictions.

When migratory trout and salmon live in a large body of water, they become bright silver in color. This is prevalent in the trout and salmon transplanted from the Pacific and Atlantic Oceans, but even native lake trout and brook trout, although retaining their identifying marks, often have a silvery hue when living in the big lake. However, cohos, chinooks, and rainbows are the species most commonly confused. Proper identification of Atlantic salmon and brown trout or brook trout and splake is tricky, too. Look for the following features to identify your catch.

Coho salmon have a dusky mouth, with the teeth set in whitish gums. The tail has some large spots, mostly in the upper half. The anal fin is long, with twelve to fifteen rays. Typically, cohos weigh less than five pounds.

Chinook salmon have a dusky mouth and gums, with a **V**-shaped lower jaw. The tail has many spots throughout. The anal fin is very long, with fifteen to nineteen rays.

mouths during the winter and spring, where they are caught by shore-casters, small-boat trollers, and ice-anglers. Skamania steelhead, stocked in limited numbers by Michigan, Wisconsin, and Minnesota, are expected to stage near tributary streams in the summer and to run the rivers during late summer and fall. Because rainbow trout wander, stray 'loopers and Skamanias may show up anywhere. Stocked rainbow trout in Lake Superior are marked with clipped fins.

Steelhead are primarily caught while they stage near river mouths before the spawn and when they run tributary streams. Although trollers occasionally find an abundance of steelhead, usually offshore,

Rainbow trout have a white mouth. The tail has many small spots in distinct rows. The anal fin is short, with nine to twelve rays. Although rainbows caught in the lake may be bright silver, those living in streams or preparing to spawn have a stripe along their flanks that ranges in color from a faint pink to vivid red.

Atlantic salmon have a forked tail with few spots. The base of the tail is narrow. The anal fin is short, with eight to eleven rays. Often, the fish have X- or cross-shaped markings on their backs. You may notice the fish has a somewhat pointed head.

Brown trout have a square tail with few spots. The base of the tail is thick. The anal fin is short, with ten to twelve rays. The body is spotted with large black, blue, and red spots, and may have small X markings.

Brook trout have a square tail. The pectoral, ventral, and anal fins are edged with white. On the flanks are small red spots edged with blue halos. Along the back are lighter-colored wormlike markings called vermiculations.

Lake trout have a deeply forked tail. Coloration varies, but markings consist of light spots on a dark background. The pectoral, ventral, and anal fins are edged with white.

Splake resemble brook trout. Sometimes even fisheries biologists have trouble distinguishing between the two species. As a rule of thumb, a fish that looks like a brook trout with a forked tail is a splake.

most often the big rainbows are an incidental trolling catch. The best steelhead fishing opportunities come during the April and May spawning run, although some large rivers receive fall runs.

Coho Salmon

Coho Salmon

When fishing for coho, look to the streams of Lake Superior's South Shore in autumn.

Many anglers say the coho salmon is the best-tasting fish swimming in the lake. A Pacific salmon species first stocked in Lake Superior in 1966, the popular coho has thrived; the lake's population now is comprised primarily of wild fish. Although small, when they're available, cohos make preferred targets for trollers. Coho fishing in any one port is seasonal because the salmon migrate throughout the lake.

Cohos have a three-year lifespan and die after they spawn. Mature cohos typically weigh about five pounds, although in winter and early spring trollers often boat immature cohos weighing less than two pounds. Voracious feeders, cohos are often caught near the surface. During the summer, a large portion of their diet consists of land-born insects blown into the lake by prevailing winds.

Stream anglers should note that cohos have distinct spawning requirements. In late autumn, they seek out tiny spring-fed tributaries, often migrating all the way upstream to headwater areas. The best spawning streams are located on the South Shore, although you can catch the odd coho from North Shore streams, too.

Chinook Salmon

Chinook Salmon

In the 1980s, thanks to successful stocking efforts, record-breaking chinook (or king) salmon were taken from Lake Superior.

Chinook (king) salmon are the broad-shouldered bruisers among Lake Superior's game fish. Reaching weights topping thirty pounds, these Pacific Ocean transplants will make the drag on your reel smoke. Pandemonium rules when a big king strikes.

Although avidly pursued by some sport anglers,

Lake Superior chinooks have never achieved the popularity nor status the species has on Lake Michigan. Early stockings by Michigan, Wisconsin, and Minnesota, in the late 1960s and 1970s, had only moderate success. The salmon were considerably smaller than their Lake Michigan counterparts and less abundant. They also proved more difficult to catch in Lake Superior's clear waters.

The 1980s was the decade of chinooks on Lake Superior. Stocking efforts started to pay off, and a fishery for both trollers and stream anglers blossomed. Records fell as chinooks increased in size, with fish weighing twenty to thirty pounds becoming common. However, some viewed this salmon bonanza with trepidation. Large spawning runs took place in rivers where chinooks had never been stocked, most notably Ontario's Nipigon and Michipicoten rivers. And some wondered what chinooks were eating to grow so large during their short five-year life span. Anglers and biologists expressed concern that voracious chinooks might damage the lake's forage base and outcompete other species.

In recent years some areas have experienced inconsistent chinook runs. Whether this is a short-term trend or an indication of change in the population remains to be seen. Chinooks are now stocked in Michigan, Wisconsin, Minnesota, and Ontario.

Pink Salmon

Pink, or humpbacked, salmon have a somewhat mythic origin. Legend has it that in 1956 a keg of pink salmon fingerlings bound for Hudson Bay tumbled off a floatplane dock in Ontario, releasing its cargo into the waters of Thunder Bay. Whatever their origin, the pink salmon became fruitful and multiplied, so that they are now present throughout the Great Lakes.

During the 1970s, large numbers of pinks

Pink Salmon

According to legend, the pink salmon was introduced to Lake Superior by accident.

made September spawning runs in Lake Superior streams. Initially the pinks, which ordinarily have a two-year life cycle, spawned only in odd-numbered years. Biologists believe that it was Superior's cold waters that delayed the maturity of enough pinks to the age of three years to establish spawning runs in even years, too. However, even though they now run every year, "humpies" have become less common. This

The Insidious Sea Lamprey

The future of Lake Superior's fishery rests with sea lamprey control. Native to the Atlantic Ocean, these parasitic eels traveled through the Great Lakes via the St. Lawrence Seaway, first arriving in Lake Ontario when the Erie Canal opened in 1819. During the 1940s they arrived in Lake Superior, and by the 1960s they had nearly wiped out lake trout and other soft-skinned species. The comeback of Lake Superior's fishery has been based on international control efforts, primarily treating spawning streams with chemical lampricides and building low weirs to prevent lamprey from swimming upstream to spawn, to keep these piscatorial parasites in check. However, sea lamprey can only be controlled, not eradicated, and ensuring adequate government funding is a constant struggle, particularly in the United States. If you hear on the news that sea lamprey control funding is in jeopardy, drop a letter to your congressional representatives and remind them that the benefits of this program far outweigh its cost.

You may catch trout and salmon that have round lamprey scars or still have the eels attached to their flanks. A sea lamprey attaches to a fish with a round mouth that has rasplike teeth. It tears open a wound and sucks the fish's body juices and may remain attached for weeks. Although not all the

victims die from the lamprey attack, annual sea lamprey mortality for lake trout on Lake Superior has been estimated as equal to the combined sport and commercial catch.

pattern of a rapid population explosion followed by a decline and leveling off is common for an exotic species introduced to a new environment.

In Lake Superior, the average pink salmon weighs less than two pounds. Although they are caught occasionally by trollers and can be caught by stream anglers when spawning, pinks are not an important sport fish. The eating quality of pink salmon deteriorates rapidly once they enter the streams to spawn. However, male spawners become impressive-looking fish, developing a pronounced humped back and distinctive kype—an extension of the lower jaw.

Atlantic Salmon

The Atlantic salmon is regarded as the world's premier sport fish, a leaping, hard-running battler that is challenging to hook. The bittersweet story of the Atlantic in Lake Superior illustrates the gap between what anglers want and what fish managers can provide. The Atlantic appears to be a species that should thrive in Lake Superior. As with rainbow trout, strains of Atlantics occur in both salt and fresh water, and Atlantics survive spawning and return to big water. Lake Ontario once had a tremendous population of landlocked Atlantics, which were driven into extinction by habitat destruction and overharvest in the nineteenth century. Even more promising, much of the Atlantic's native habitat resembles Lake Superior's environment. So why hasn't the Atlantic salmon thrived in Lake Superior and the other Great Lakes?

Certainly, fish managers have tried. Atlantics have been stocked in the Great Lakes for over a century, but stocking returns were typically poor. Minnesota made the news in 1992 when the state Department of Natural Resources announced it

Atlantic Salmon

Regarded as the world's premier sport fish, Atlantic salmon in Lake Superior average over ten pounds and are known to put up a strong fight.

was discontinuing a costly and unsuccessful stocking program on Lake Superior—shortly before anglers started catching them in unprecedented numbers. At present, Atlantics are an occasional catch in Lake Superior. Although they may show up anywhere, you are most likely to catch Atlantics within seventy-five miles of Duluth-Superior. However, another stocking program shows promise at the St. Marys River, Lake Superior's outlet, where Atlantics that live in Lake Huron and perhaps Lake Superior are making spawning runs.

Lake Superior Atlantic salmon are strong fighters that can weigh ten pounds or more. Those found in the St. Marys River are even bigger. Typically, Atlantics are found in the spring and early summer, around river mouths and in nearshore waters where they are available to shore-casters and small-boat trollers. They run the rivers in spring, late summer, and fall. Finding them in the streams is a happenstance occurrance.

Brown Trout

Don't underestimate the brown trout. They often evade even the most skillful anglers.

Brown Trout

Brown trout are European immigrants that first arrived in the Lake Superior drainage over a century ago. Today they are most common along the South Shore, where Michigan and Wisconsin stock them. Browns typically grow to larger sizes than steelhead, exceeding ten and occasionally twenty pounds.

Brown trout are not pushovers. Nocturnal and wary, they often evade all but the most skillful or lucky anglers. They can be caught by trolling or by fishing in the streams or through the ice. The best times to catch them by trolling are in spring, early summer, and late summer. August and September are good months for stream fishing. In places like Chequamegon Bay, browns can be caught through the ice.

Burbot

Burbot

Every winter on Minnesota's Leech Lake, the community of Walker sponsors an Eelpout Festival, an ice-fishing contest for one of the ugliest fish swimming in northern waters—the burbot, or eelpout. A close cousin to the saltwater cod, the homely burbot is native to large lakes, including Lake Superior. Here most anglers call them lawyers. Look a burbot in the eye and use your imagination to speculate on the origin of that name. Perhaps the burbot's tendency to wrap around your arm when you try to unhook it has something to do with its lack of popularity among anglers. However, not everyone looks askance at the lowly lawyer. Growing numbers of anglers are discovering that burbot taste great.

> The burbot —or eelpout— is one of the ugliest fish swimming in northern waters.

Burbot prefer deepwater habitat, and, as with lake trout, populations of this soft–skinned fish were decimated by invading sea lampreys. However, burbot populations increased following lamprey control efforts. Most often they are caught through the ice by anglers fishing for lake trout. In some places, such as Superior's Nemadji River, anglers fish for burbot when they spawn in midwinter.

The Whitefish

Lake Superior has two species of whitefish: lake whitefish and round whitefish (menominee). Although neither is an important sport species, both can be caught on hook and line and are good to eat. In some places, such as along the Upper Peninsula and in the St. Marys River, sport fisheries exist. Lake whitefish are an especially exciting quarry for fly-casters during the summer mayfly hatches.

Lake Whitefish

> During the summer mayfly hatches, lake whitefish challenge fly-casters.

The lake whitefish, the larger of the two species, historically reached weights topping forty pounds in Lake Superior. However, overfishing, pollution, and sea lamprey depredation led to

*Round Whitefish
(Menominee)*

Smoked menomonie
are a local delicacy.

declines in both size and numbers of lake white-fish. Today they are found primarily in locations along the South Shore and in Ontario waters.

Menominee are small, averaging about one pound in size. They are often found in coastal waters, where anglers fishing with small baits occasionally catch them. Like their larger cousins, menominee are excellent when smoked.

Lake Herring, Etc.

In recent years, Superior's native lake herring populations have rebounded, especially in the western end of the lake. This is good news for both sport anglers and netters because the herring provides a vital link in the food chain and is an important commercial species. You can find fresh and smoked herring for sale in grocery stores around the lake, and many local restaurants feature herring on the menu.

Nuisance Exotics

While some exotic species, such as the Pacific salmon, are prized by anglers, others threaten the lake's piscatorial balance. Sea lamprey, of course, have had a major impact on Superior's fishery. A number of other exotic species have also made their way to the lake—usually because of human error.

A good example is the river ruffe, a small perch-like Eurasian fish that probably was "stocked" into the Duluth-Superior harbor when an ocean freighter dumped ballast water. The ruffe has done so well in its new home that fish managers have lowered the bag limits on predator game fish and increased stockings in an attempt to control them. Superior's icy waters have prevented the ruffe from spreading in the lake.

Cold water has also controlled another exotic, the zebra mussel. These tiny clams pose an enormous problem on the lower Great Lakes, where they cover spawning reefs and clog water intake lines. Although small colonies have been discovered in Superior, zebra mussels do not seem to be increasing.

During the 1930s and 1940s, lakewide netting harvests of herring ran from fifteen to nearly twenty million pounds. However, the herring population plummeted during the 1960s and 1970s. No one is sure why, but scientists theorize that overfishing, competition and predation from smelt, and perhaps the biological imbalance caused by the crash of the lake's fish populations, are probable reasons. During the 1980s herring numbers started to increase, while smelt populations declined. The herring's return may mean the lake's fishery is beginning to recover. It may also mean anglers will have to learn new tactics. Herring live in large schools in the open lake. Trollers may have to travel miles offshore in order to locate fish.

Related to herring, but less important to the anglers, are the chubs, which primarily live in deep offshore waters. About the only place anglers will encounter them is at a smoked fish shop.

Lake Herring

The population of native lake herring has risen in recent years.

However, biologists worry that the species could spread to inland lakes.

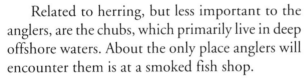

Carp, enthusiastically stocked throughout the United States in the late nineteenth century, are present in shallow bays and some river systems around the lake. Occasionally, you'll see small schools of cruising carp near the surface. Generally, cold water temps keep the carp population in check and prevent it from expanding to nuisance levels.

A tiny water flea called *bythotrephes cederstromi* or, more simply, B.C., is a native of the Caspian Sea that arrived in the Great Lakes in the 1980s. It feeds on the same plankton as do small fish and can disrupt food chains. Anglers occasionally find the water fleas clumped on fishing lines and downrigger cables. Another traveler, the rusty crayfish, has appeared in the Pigeon River and some other streams. This crayfish has a massive appetite for aquatic weeds and can displace native crayfish species.

Rainbow Smelt

As the population of the once-plentiful rainbow smelt has declined, so have local beer sales during the smelt's annual spring run.

Rainbow Smelt

Rainbow smelt are another exotic species that arrived in Lake Superior more or less by accident. First stocked in a Michigan inland lake early in this century, the small, silvery fish made their way to Lake Michigan and then to Lake Superior. The diminutive size of smelt, which average six to eleven inches in length, belies their predatory nature. Many commercial netters blame the demise of Great Lakes whitefish and herring on smelt, which prey on the young of both species.

Smelt populations in Lake Superior peaked during the years native fish populations crashed. In fact, during the 1950s to 1970s, dipnetting for spawning smelt when they ran tributary streams in the spring was one of the largest recreational fisheries on the lake. Since smelt mostly run the streams at night, smelting evolved into a weird spring rite that required bonfires, people willing to bite the heads off fresh-caught smelt, and gallons of beer. Smelt populations throughout the lake began to falter during the 1980s, perhaps due to the growing numbers of predator fish in the lake.

Smelt, an important forage species, live in the top two-hundred feet of water. This means that the fish that are feeding on them are accessible to trollers. As smelt numbers have declined, game fish habits seem to have changed. For instance, although lake trout still congregate off river mouths in the spring, they seem to show up later than they once did—perhaps because the schools of spawning smelt that provided an earlier food source are no longer available.

Walleye

Pollution and over-fishing destroyed populations of this popular game fish.

Walleye

Walleyes are game fish of importance in some areas of Lake Superior. They usually are found near large river estuaries and bays, which provide spawning and feeding habitat. Some walleye populations have been destroyed by pollution and overfishing. On the Nipigon River efforts are underway to restore the walleye population. Once so numerous they were considered a nuisance, the walleyes were wiped out by pollution. In the 1980s, pollution control on the St. Louis River led to a rediscovery of the river's trophy walleyes. Anglers pursue walleyes both in the river and on the open lake.

Northern Pike

Northern Pike

Fishing pressure has greatly reduced the number of trophy pike in Lake Superior.

Most anglers say that Lake Superior northern pike fishing just ain't what it used to be. The giant northerns that patrolled estuaries and shallow areas as recently as ten years ago have been greatly reduced in numbers. In places such as Chequamegon Bay, fishing pressure is the culprit. Lake Superior has a limited amount of northern pike habitat and can produce only small numbers of trophy fish. Even a few anglers can damage the population. Northerns weighing twenty pounds or more can still be caught in places like the St. Louis River estuary. Do the fish and the future a favor: practice catch-and-release.

Smallmouth Bass

Smallmouth Bass

"Pound for pound, the gamest fish that swims."

Because Lake Superior is so cold and deep, it contains very little smallmouth bass habitat. However, a high-quality smallmouth bass fishery exists in Chequamegon Bay, and the species occurs in Batchawana Bay and tributary streams like the St. Louis and Kaministiquia Rivers. Superior's outflow, the St. Marys River, also offers excellent smallmouth fishing.

The smallmouth has been called "pound for pound, the gamest fish that swims." A hardened steelheader might disagree, but few would deny that the smallmouth is a fighter. Generally found in waters less than twenty-five feet deep, smallmouth are easily accessible to light-tackle anglers. In Lake Superior tributaries, they spawn during May and June, and as late as July during cold summers. The best fishing comes during the summer months, when warm water temperatures activate the smallmouth's metabolism.

Lake Sturgeon

Lake Sturgeon

Lake Superior's largest fish can reach lengths of six feet and weigh over one hundred pounds.

The largest fish swimming in Lake Superior is undoubtedly a lake sturgeon. The slow-growing lake sturgeon can reach lengths of six feet, weigh over one hundred pounds, and can live to reach the century-mark. Unfortunately, the sturgeon was despised by early commercial netters, who caught the giant fish and then piled them like cordwood on the shore. Superior's sturgeon populations never recovered from such wanton destruction. However, fish managers have begun stocking sturgeon in areas where they were once abundant, in hopes of restoring the species.

Yellow Perch

Yellow Perch

The walleye's smaller cousin, yellow perch are yet another Lake Superior native on the decline.

Yellow perch are the walleye's smaller cousin, a fish found tasty by both anglers and game fish. Unfortunately, yellow perch populations in Superior just aren't what they used to be. Heavy sport-fishing pressure has reduced the size and numbers of perch in Chequamegon Bay, and intense commercial netting has affected the yellow perch fishery in Michigan's Whitefish Bay. Perch are also found in the St. Louis River and Batchawana Bay, as well as other areas that support species such as walleyes and northern pike.

Shore Fishing

MANY ANGLERS FIRST MEET Lake Superior while standing on its shore armed with a spinning rod and a heavy spoon. The lake's immensity overwhelms, and the chance of actually catching something seems minuscule. Nevertheless, shore-casting provides an inexpensive, accessible, and effective way to become acquainted with the lake and the fish it contains.

Beginners will find that an inland spinning rod and reel combo spooled with 6- to 10-pound-test monofilament is sufficient, even though serious shore-anglers use customized tackle. Spoons and spinners for shore-casting are available at every shoreline fishing shop. Ask the clerk to show you the local favorites, and then pick out another spoon or two that strikes your fancy. This is, after all, fishing, not brain surgery.

Beginners will find that an inland spinning rod and reel combo spooled with 6- to 10-pound-test monofilament is sufficient, even though serious shore-anglers use customized tackle.

Right Time, Right Place

Successful shore-casting is very much a matter of being in the right place at the right time under the right conditions. Trout and salmon frequent shoreline areas at specific times of year. You must know when the fish are there, what conditions are best suited to fishing, and how to catch them.

Novices are often stymied about their inability to catch fish when a nearby experienced angler is getting action. In those situations, you should pay attention to the experienced angler's fishing technique and heed any advice the angler might offer. Remember, though, that anglers are a funny breed. Some share secrets, others fib, and a few are plain unfriendly.

Finding good places to shore-cast is easy, because anglers have good shoreline access all around the lake. The most popular places are river mouths, piers, breakwalls, and areas with good shoreline structure, such as submerged boulders or adjacent deep water. Few hot spots are secret. When the fishing is good, you'll usually see other anglers. In fact, some of the more popular places can get crowded.

Fishing in crowds can be productive when the fish are staging near spawning areas, but seeking solitude is usually a wiser shore-casting option. Trout and salmon are spooky critters. The unnatural sounds of human activity can scare them away. Even when fishing alone, be sneaky and quiet. Often you'll be casting in shallow, very clear water. Don't advertise your presence with heavy footsteps, unnecessary wading, or sloppy fishing technique.

Remember, too, that trout and salmon become wary when in shallow water because they are exposed to predators, including you. Usually the fish are most likely to enter shallow water areas during low-light periods, such as dawn and dusk or overcast days. A chop on the water helps keep the fish near shore throughout the day, but a heavy surf makes shore-fishing impossible.

Of course, the right fishing conditions are only one-half of the equation; the fish must be there, too. Be prepared to hear "you should'a been here

Fishing in crowds can be productive when the fish are staging near spawning areas, but seeking solitude is usually a wiser shore-casting option.

yesterday" often when you're learning the ropes, especially if you're chasing chinooks or steelhead. Lake trout are generally more consistent.

Shore-casters frequent different places at various times of year. In the spring, casters gather at river mouths to fish for rainbow trout preparing to make their spawning runs. Smelt also spawn in the spring, attracting hungry lake trout and salmon. Because the river water is usually warmer than that of the lake, these species remain near river mouths until early summer.

When the summer sun finally warms Superior's ever-frigid water, you can cast for lake trout and other species from breakwalls, points, or piers. Look for areas with access to nearby deep water. The fish will be most active when the water temperature is between forty-eight and sixty degrees. Carry a thermometer and check the water temp before making your first cast. If the water is too cold, get in your vehicle and hopscotch along the shoreline until you find suitable temperatures. Sometimes the water temperature shows surprising variation in just a short distance along the shoreline.

As summer progresses and the trout and salmon move offshore to forage, shore-casters may have a lull in the action. However, the truly adventurous can seek out alternative species, such as northern pike. Some large estuaries and shallow bays harbor at least small populations of northern pike. But the size of the populations has no bearing on the size of the fish. Trophies have been taken, although less frequently in recent years, at Duluth-Superior, Ashland, and Marquette.

Autumn's first cool breezes draw to the shoreline another brawler, the mighty chinook. Perhaps the most light-sensitive of any Lake Superior sport fish, chinooks are often taken before sunup and

Sometimes the water temperature shows surprising variation in just a short distance along the shoreline.

The Mighty Chinook

after sundown in the vicinity of river mouths. Although chinooks ascend virtually every sizable tributary, you'll find the best numbers off streams that are stocked or have established wild runs. Be prepared to put some time in. Chinooks preparing to spawn are fickle biters. Just because you can see them porpoising off the river mouth doesn't mean they'll strike.

Cast with tiny spoons and spinners near river mouths in early September and you may catch pink salmon. When caught in the lake, these small fish retain their silvery color and are good to eat. Their edible quality diminishes quickly once they enter the stream. If you are truly fortunate, you might catch a brook trout, or on the South Shore it could be a splake, preparing to spawn. Atlantic salmon are another infrequent, but exciting, catch.

When the leaves begin to fall, lake trout move in to spawn along beaches and reefs. In some locations you can find immense concentrations of easy-to-catch fish—so easy, in fact, that lake trout fishing seasons are often closed in the fall to protect these vulnerable fish. Because these spawning fish represent the future of Lake Superior fishing, it is wise to practice catch-and-release.

Shore-fishing opportunities are limited during the winter, with the exception of the Kamloops

No Wire Leaders!

Unless you are fishing specifically for northern pike, never use a wire leader. Why? First, trout, salmon, and walleyes don't have the dental equipment necesary to bite through your line. If your line breaks, undoubtedly it is because the fish surged against a tight drag, the line was frayed, or a poorly tied knot came undone. Second, the heavy leader detracts from the action of your lure and is visible to line-wary fish. Use a snap swivel instead to make lure changes easier and prevent line twist.

fishery on Minnesota's coast. These chunky rainbow trout cruise the shoreline shallows throughout the winter and are very popular with area anglers. 'Looper devotees also catch occasional steelhead, cohos, and lake trout. Although this isn't a sport for fair-weather anglers, many winter days are surprisingly pleasant. The lake's open water moderates the climate, so that air temperatures may be substantially warmer on the shore than a few miles inland.

Kamloops
Rainbow Trout

The Art of Artificials

Heaving a spoon isn't as easy as it first appears. Beginners soon learn the lake bottom has an insatiable appetite for expensive lures. In fact, sometimes it seems you'd be better off throwing a fistful of dollar bills into the lake and walking away. Scuba divers have a successful cottage industry in recovering lost spoons and selling them back to anglers. However, most casters quickly learn to begin their retrieve immediately and keep the rod tip high to avoid hangups. When casting into deep water, such as off a breakwall, you can use a countdown method to get your lure near the bottom. Expect to lose a spoon or two while mastering this technique.

Most casters quickly learn to begin their retrieve immediately and keep the rod tip high to avoid hangups.

Casting spoons come in various weights and styles. Some are long and slender, others short and wide. You can cast heavy spoons, those weighing a half ounce or more, the greatest distance, but they sink rapidly. Lighter spoons may not go as far, but allow you more variation in your retrieve. Of course, the action of any spoon changes with the speed of the retrieve. Make a few test runs at your feet to determine the proper speed. Many shore-casters find that varying the speed of retrieve or incorporating the pull-and-flutter-down action of jigging induces more strikes. Lake trout are

Casting Spoons

especially susceptible to the wounded-baitfish appearance of a jigged spoon.

Although you can purchase casting spoons in many color combinations, a few old standbys produce the most fish. Choose colors such as silver, fluorescent green, or orange, blue, white, and gold. Prism tape and luminescent (glow) markings are also effective. Often, a particular color combination or spoon style is hot. Pay attention to what successful anglers are using and how they fish.

In some places, you'll see that the people catching fish are casting spinners. Some anglers prefer using spinners, especially when fishing in river mouth currents. Spinners with weighted bodies and feather or bucktail skirts are most effective and the easiest to cast. When casting with spinners, be sure to use a quality ball-bearing swivel to prevent line twist. White and chartreuse are favorite colors.

Spinner with Bucktail Skirt

Stick baits also account for their share of fish. Jointed plugs, which have more action, get the nod from serious shore-casters. Floating stick baits, though effective, are difficult to cast. You can add casting weight without impairing the action by pinching a heavy split shot to your line about eighteen inches ahead of the lure. Another trick that will let you outdistance a pro caster is to float your plug out from shore with the river current. Pay out line at the same speed as the drifting plug to avoid developing loops of slack. Some patience is required, but the distance you gain is worth any lost casting time. Slowly retrieve the plug against the current.

Jointed Plug

Bait and Wait

Patience, they say, is a virtue. Just ask anyone who has ever sat on a muddy riverbank fishing for catfish. You cast out a gob of smelly bait, then sit back and wait for a hungry catfish to find it. In many ways, trout and salmon are similar to catfish. They often feed on the bottom, and scent attracts them to their prey (or bait). In fact, most catfish baits—with the possible exception of rotten chicken liver—will catch trout and salmon, too

Lake Superior bait slingers must contend with rocky bottoms and wave action. In some places you'll hang up on virtually every cast, especially if the surf pulls on your line. If the lake is calm, you can fish with a float. However, in many situations you'll be bottom fishing. The trick is to float your bait off the bottom and use a snag-proof sinker system.

Floating the bait is easy. You can use an air-inflated nightcrawler as you would when fishing for walleyes, or you can add foam floats or one-half a miniature marshmallow to your spawn sack for buoyancy. When fishing a sand or cobble-stone bottom, you can get by with a walking sinker. However, if the bottom is more rugged, use a dropper system. Attach a small barrel swivel to your main line, then run a leader to your hook. Tie a short dropper line to the swivel. Pinch on your sinkers to the dropper. If the sinkers hang up, they'll slide off the dropper when you tug on the line.

Some baits are especially well suited to bobber-fishing. Many anglers suspend a small marabou jig tipped with a wax worm beneath a tiny float when fishing for Kamloops rainbows. Other popular rainbow baits include mayfly wigglers, stonefly nymphs, nightcrawlers, and spawn. A small minnow on a plain hook will catch just about anything that swims in the lake, although it is sometimes less effective than other baits. Live shiner or sucker minnows still-fished beneath a

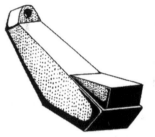

Walking Sinker

Dropper System

bobber can be the ticket for northern pike or lake trout. Lake whitefish, menominee and lake herring can be caught with waxworms, maggots, and single salmon eggs.

When to fish bait? Anytime you fish near river mouths, bait is a viable option. In the spring, try drifting spawn sacks in the current at the river mouth. When the smelt are running, or even later in the year, you can catch lake trout and salmon using dead smelt. However, fishing with dead smelt is often more trouble than it is worth. Unless they are very fresh, smelt are soft and difficult to keep on the hook. Burbot, seagulls, and mergansers also find this bait very attractive. Still-fishing with bait accounts for many shore-caught chinooks each fall. Try floating a spawn sack or nightcrawler off the bottom at dawn or dusk. When you get a strike, quickly set the hook.

Belly Boats

Most spoon slingers eventually get tired of standing on the beach. You can heave a spoon only so far. Often it seems the fish are nearby, but just beyond reach. A pair of chest waders extends your range somewhat, but not enough. If you could only get out another one-hundred feet...

In these situations a belly boat, or float tube, is the ticket. A belly boat is an inflatable tube with a nylon shell and a fabric sling for a seat. A belly boater sits in the tube while wearing chest waders and propels the tiny craft by kicking with swim fins. It's a surprisingly comfortable way to fish and one that allows you to approach within casting range of wary, shallow-water trout or salmon that would spook away from a boat.

A belly boat provides an affordable and fun way to fish Lake Superior. Fly-casters find it especially helpful, because it greatly increases the amount of water they can cover. Battling a sizable fish from a float tube is a memorable

Rods and Reels

Shore anglers around the lake have developed customized tackle to meet their needs. An off-the-rack spinning rod is just fine for walleye or crappie fishing, but has some shortcomings for Lake Superior anglers. The average spinning rod has neither the length nor backbone necessary for long-distance casts, and makes an inadequate tool for playing large, powerful fish. And an inexpensive reel may not stand up to a fast-running chinook or steelhead.

Most shore-anglers prefer custom-built graphite rods eight to ten feet in length. The extra length (the average spinning rod is six or seven feet) increases casting distance, provides more sensitivity, and facilitates playing big fish on light line. Such rods should be built with top-quality guides spaced at proper intervals so that the line follows the contours of a bowed rod. Some anglers build rods with

experience, because the fish can tow you about. Novices should think about how they will land, unhook, and store their catch before they hook a fish. Forget to take along a landing net and a stringer, and catching a five-pound lake trout from a belly boat can quickly become a one-ring circus.

Of course, venturing out on unpredictable Lake Superior in such a craft requires common sense and respect for the lake. Avoid windy days, river currents, and areas with boat traffic. The belly boat should be used for fishing nearshore areas in calm weather. *Always* wear a life preserver, and *never* take chances. Lake Superior allows little room for error.

*Spinning Rod
and Reel*

a cork grip and no reel seat, using tape to attach the reel to the rod. This allows the rod to bend fully into the butt and gives you an extra edge of sensitivity when fishing with bait. And on cold days the cork grip is much warmer than a metal reel seat.

Are these long rods what Great Lakes anglers call noodle rods? Not necessarily. A noodle rod has a very soft action so anglers can play fish on very light line, such as 2-pound test. The soft action is fine for fishing with bait, but too wimpy for casting spoons. Casters need a stiff-action rod to work their lures with the proper action and be able to set the hook in the hard mouth of a trout or salmon. When choosing a shore-fishing rod, be sure the action is suited to your fishing style.

Choosing a spinning reel is easier. Look for one with enough spool capacity to hold two-hundred yards of 6- or 8-pound-test monofilament line. Be sure it has a smooth running drag and is geared for high-speed retrieves. The best models have no knobs, bolts, or other doodads near the bail that can catch your line. Spool your reel with a quality low-visibility monofilament testing eight pounds or less. In the open waters of the lake, heavy line isn't necessary to play and land big fish.

What about bait-casting or spin-casting rigs? Avoid them. Both are designed for fishing situations other than those you are likely to encounter on the Great Lakes. The short, stiff rods are not designed to cast long distances nor control large, powerful fish. Exceptions, of course, are trolling outfits and drift rigs, although neither is suited to shore-casting.

Fly-Casting Fun

Growing numbers of shore anglers are discovering that fly-casting is an exciting and productive way to fish. In fact, if you can approach within close range of trout and salmon in shallow water or near the surface, a well-placed fly makes an extremely effective presentation. Yes, you can handle these powerful fish on a fly rod, but expect a heck of a tussle before they reach the net.

The Lake Superior fly-fishing tradition reaches back to the wealthy sports who traveled to the Nipigon and the Brule during the 1800s to fish for brook trout, yet it also presents an untapped frontier for intrepid anglers. During the twentieth century both Lake Superior and fly-fishing have changed. The lake now supports a wide array of species willing to take a fly, and technological advancements in fly-fishing tackle make it possible to fish flies from the surface to depths of thirty feet or more.

The greatest stumbling block facing a fledgling Lake Superior fly-caster is to be there when the fish swim within casting range. As always, the big lake calls the shots. A strong surf, cold water, or some other natural condition can make fly-fishing either impossible or a complete waste of time. Weekend anglers should plan their trips for the best times and have a viable Plan B (fishing inland lakes or streams) ready in case Superior throws a curve. Generally speaking, the best opportunities for fly-fishers come when trout and salmon are available to shore-casters or small-boat trollers.

Although you'll be fishing for big fish, don't arm yourself with tarpon tackle. A 7-weight fly rod will suffice in most situations, and a rod larger than 9-weight is overkill. Use a fly reel with a reliable drag and the spool capacity to hold two hundred yards of backing.

The type of fly line you use is important. Floating lines, commonly used by stream anglers, are affected by waves, which makes it difficult to

Keep Your Hooks Sharp!

Experienced anglers carry a small file or other honing device and fastidiously sharpen their hooks. Trout and salmon have hard mouths and hook setting is difficult enough even when your hooks are razor-sharp.
Make a habit of frequently touching up your hooks— even on new lures.

impart the proper action when retrieving a fly. Experts suggest using an intermediate-weight or slow-sinking fly line so that you have direct contact with the submerged fly. Avoid sink-tip fly lines, which present the same problem as floaters. A fast-sinking line can be used to fish deeper water. Clear-colored lines are less likely to disturb the fish. Although a good fly-caster will catch more fish than a poor one, you don't have to be long-distance champ to fly-fish Lake Superior. Fly-casters either wade or use belly boats to get within casting range.

Favorite Flies

All the critters eaten by Lake Superior trout and salmon can be imitated with flies. In fact, the world-famous Muddler Minnow originated as an imitation of sculpin minnows found in the Nipigon River. Generally speaking, minnow-imitating streamer patterns are most versatile, but the well-stocked fly-caster will carry some nymphs and dry flies, too. Stream anglers and shoreline fly-casters discovered that early spring rainbows have a taste for nymphs. During the summer, you may find that trout and salmon feeding on the surface can be enticed with dry flies.

Many patterns that fly-casters find productive are all-purpose flies that work well in other waters. Simple nymph patterns such as the Hare's Ear, Pheasant Tail, and Brassy from size 10 to tiny size 18 are effective in river-mouth currents. In the spring and fall, try egg patterns fashioned from yarn. Wooly Buggers in brown, olive, and black tied in various sizes prove effective in a range of conditions. Feather streamers, such as the Lefty's Deceiver, imitate bait fish. Some anglers tie their streamers on bend-back hooks so that the hook point rides upright to minimize hang-ups. If you

Muddler Minnow

Hare's Ear

Wooly Bugger

Lefty's Deceiver

fish dry flies, try to match the insect that the fish are eating. Blind-casting with a dry fly when you see no surface activity is a lesson in futility.

Also, try using small flies and light tippets. Lake Superior is clear, cold, and inhospitable to aquatic life, so trout and salmon—even big ones—often feed on small morsels. Anglers who tie their own flies will find a fly-fishing frontier on Lake Superior. Don't be afraid to experiment. If at first you don't succeed, keep at it. When the fish are within your casting range, you can find ways to catch them.

Muskrat Nymph

Small Boat Trolling

LAKE SUPERIOR HAS WAYS OF making you feel insignificant, and none know this better than small boaters. After all, this lake sometimes challenges even freighters and ore ships. Yet centuries before the St. Lawrence Seaway was constructed, canoes provided transportation on the lake. At Grand Portage, Minnesota, a cedar tree at least four hundred years old clings to a shoreline rock—mute veteran of centuries of storms and winters. Early European explorers reported that native people left offerings there before making the twenty-mile passage to Isle Royale in bark canoes. Later the voyageurs left offerings when they headed for Montreal in freighter canoes laden with fur.

If you are careful, you can use a canoe or small inland boat on Lake Superior. Although the lake sometimes gets as rough as an ocean, on many days it is calm enough for small craft. If you respect the lake and the limitations of your craft, you can have good fishing. Only a fool takes chances, because the sailors say Lake Superior never gives up her dead.

Although small-boat anglers can't venture very far offshore, they do have some advantages over anglers in larger craft. You can launch a small boat just about anywhere you have access to the

Although the lake sometimes gets as rough as an ocean, on many days it is calm enough for small craft.

lake—particularly helpful during the winter when launch ramps are closed. You can fish in shallow water with less likelihood of spooking wary fish or damaging an expensive (and unrowable) boat. And you can use your inland fishing tackle. Trolling from a small boat makes an excellent starting point for anglers who wish to get serious about Lake Superior fishing—you can learn the ropes before choosing and purchasing a larger Lake Superior rig.

Although you can outfit fourteen- and sixteen-foot boats with downriggers, planer boards, and other trolling gear, this chapter focuses on how to use a typical inland rig on the big lake.

Use Trustworthy Equipment

Not just *any* small boat will do for fishing on Lake Superior. Flat-bottomed craft such as johnboats, for instance, are designed for shallow streams and marshes, not for trolling on the world's largest lake. And this certainly isn't the place to try out the outboard you discovered among the junk in Uncle Fred's garage.

What Line?

The average inland angler uses 8-pound-test monofilament line on a spinning reel, which is sufficient for most small-boat trolling situations. However, you may want to spin some mono better suited for trolling on your reel's spare spool. A troller wants a strong, abrasion-resistant, and fairly stiff line that can stand up to abuse. The constant pull of a lure stretches and fatigues line, and the lure's action causes line twist. What pound-test? For a medium-weight spinning rig, use 8- to 12-pound line. You don't need the heavy line for battling fish. On the lake's open waters, you can play large fish on light line.

The point is that you must use reliable gear suited to big water. A fourteen-foot, V-hull aluminum boat will get you around, but a sixteen-footer is even better. Use an outboard that starts every time. Carry a small outboard or electric trolling motor for backup. On Lake Superior, often no one will be around to tow you to shore if you have engine trouble.

The law requires you to have approved life preservers for everyone on board, but only an idiot would go out without them. Regardless of the weather, bring rain gear and warm clothing. An emergency kit with tools, a powerful flashlight, extra rope, and even signal flares may save your life. Don't forget a compass, because Lake Superior fog can be as thick as pea soup.

If you plan to fish from a canoe or twelve-foot boat, go only during the calmest weather and don't venture very far from shore. Even when calm, Superior has swells that can tip unwary canoers. A nasty chop can rise quickly with just a slight breeze. Sea kayaks, although not designed for fishing, are a better choice for paddlers, because they are exceptionally seaworthy and fun to paddle.

Choosing Your Gear

You don't need a vast amount of tackle to fish the big pond, but you do need the right stuff. Leave your plastic worms, leech rigs, and spinnerbaits at home. Instead bring spoons (the ones you use for shore-casting will do) and stick baits—long, lean plugs. Mount some rod holders on the gunwales (you can make your own from PVC pipe) so you can troll in comfort. Carry a cooler with some ice in it to store the fish you catch. A long-handled net makes it easier to land them.

A fish-finder that can make soundings to one-hundred feet or more is essential. If the unit does

Be Prepared!

Regardless of the weather, make sure your craft is equipped with:

- life preservers
- rain gear
- warm clothing
- an emergency kit
- a compass

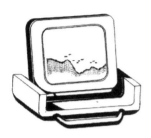

Portable Fish Finder

not have a built-in surface temperature gauge, bring a fishing thermometer. Often it is more important to know the water temperature than to know the depth. However, the fish-finder can show you bottom contours, schools of baitfish, and occasionally game fish. But don't be surprised if you read few game fish on the screen. If the trout and salmon are suspended near the surface, as they often are when you're fishing from a small boat, they may scatter when you pass over them.

Longlines, Flatlines

When you fish in shallow or clear water, trout and salmon near the surface may spook away from your boat. In fact, fly-casters and other shallow-water trout anglers often find the fish seem to stay just outside of casting range. Fortunately, fish have short memories, and they'll move back into an area after a troller has passed. This is what makes long-lining effective.

Long-lining is simply the technique of running your lures far behind the boat. Whether or not fish swim away when a boat goes by and then swim back to be fooled by the lure is open to debate, but the fact remains that long-lining works. When trolling in a small boat, let out fifty yards or more of line. Release the line slowly as you troll so that your lure doesn't sink immediately to the bottom and hang up. Make slow, wide turns for the same purpose.

If the lure you troll is unencumbered by weight and therefore is near the surface, the technique is called flat-lining. Most casual Lake Superior anglers will find this is an easy and effective way to fish. In fact, most often when trout and salmon are accessible to small boaters they are near shore or close to the surface—and catchable on flatlines. Even serious trollers often run at least one flatline behind the boat. Certain fish, such as steelhead or coho, are often near the surface; running a flatline with a favorite lure lets you catch the odd surface-oriented fish often enough to make it worthwhile.

From Sinkers to Downriggers

Although you can catch fish by trolling your lures near the surface, often the fish are farther down. You can get your lures to run deeper using sinkers, diving weights, lead-core line, or downriggers. If you're just getting started, purchase some keel sinkers. These keel-shaped weights are well suited to use with typical inland spinning tackle. Keel sinkers, which are molded to a bead chain snap to minimize line twist, come in a variety of sizes, from one-quarter ounce to two ounces or more. Tie the keel sinker to your line and then run a two-foot monofilament leader to the lure. Keel sinkers allow you to reach depths of twenty feet or more.

Keel Sinker

Heavy bottom-walking sinkers—three ounces or more—will pull your bait to thirty feet or deeper. These sinkers come in several designs, all incorporating a lead weight molded on a stiff wire to prevent it from hanging up. Use a sturdy rod and a level-wind reel spooled with strong line.

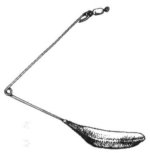

Bottom Walking Sinker

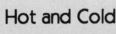

Hot and Cold

Ask tackle store clerks and charter captains about the best baits to use on Lake Superior, and they'll give you different answers from day to day or year to year. "Hot" lures change with the whims of fish and those who fish for them. A particular lure may knock 'em dead one summer and be useless the next. That's why charter captains carry a selection of baits in assorted colors. However, most will tell you that hot green (chartreuse), purple, and silver are consistent fish-catching colors.

Diver

Divers plane downward in the water and then run at a consistent depth. The weight is set to trip when a fish strikes so you can reel it in. You'll find several brands available at tackle shops. Divers give you more control over the line than keel sinkers and allow you to easily fish to depths of thirty feet or more.

Lead-core line is a weighted line marked in different colors. You control the lure's depth by the number of colors you let out. A special heavy-weight rod and a level-wind reel are used when fishing with lead-core. The heavy line saps the fight out of fish, especially smaller ones. However, fishing with a lead-core line provides an effective and inexpensive way to reach fish at depths of forty feet or more.

The most common piece of deepwater trolling gear is the downrigger. Small boat anglers can find a number of inexpensive, portable models. With portable downriggers, you can fish to depths of about one-hundred feet. (See chapter seven, "Deepwater Fishing," for a discussion on downrigging techniques.)

Downrigger

Spoons and Stick-baits

Trolling spoons come in an array of shapes and sizes, from lightweight flutter spoons to heavy hammered metals. Generally speaking, spoons require a faster trolling speed that will seem mighty quick to the average walleye angler. Pull the spoon along next to the boat to see how it's running before paying out line. Vary the spoons you show the fish until you find out what works. Try varying your presentation, too. Trolling in a zigzag pattern or making frequent turns changes the lure speed, so the spoons flutter downward on the turns and pull upward when you straighten out. Lake trout often strike spoons as they fall. In fact, old-timers use a jigging motion as they troll to impart more action in the spoon.

Don't troll spoons and stick baits at the same time because many stick baits are designed to be trolled at slower speeds. These are long, minnow-shaped lures made of wood or synthetic materials. Just behind the head is a cupped lip that gives the lure its action. The size and shape of the lip and the lure's weight determine how deep the lure will run and what will be the most effective trolling speed. Some stick baits are jointed, which increases their action.

Stick Bait

When using stick baits, always check the lure alongside the boat to see if it runs true. Often you must tune the plug by adjusting the connecting eye to get the best lure action. You may also find that some stick baits are fickle performers when the trolling speed changes. Some models are designed to run at faster speeds.

When to Fish

Unequipped to venture far from the launch in search of fish, the small-boater must wait until the fish are both accessible and present in suffi-cient numbers to make it worth going out. The local charter captain's tremendous success catch-ing lake trout by bottom bouncing in 150-foot depths doesn't mean you'll catch anything by troll-ing flatlines along the shoreline.

Generally, you're looking for conditions that bring active fish near shore and close to the sur-face. In the spring, you might anchor and cast in the flume of a river mouth. During the summer, you may find trout and salmon feeding near the surface. In some places, such as Two Harbors, Min-nesota, you can even catch cohos throughout the winter trolling from a small boat.

Be sure, however, to base your fishing trip on

something more than a whim. Newcomers to Lake Superior should do their homework and get reliable fishing information before planning a trip. At most ports, small-boaters have the best luck at specific times of year. Ask what baits are popular and how to fish them. Also inquire about the weather. It may be sweltering elsewhere in the Midwest and darned near wintery on the big lake.

Outfitting a Lake Superior Rig

STAY IN THE LAKE SUPERIOR fishing game long enough and eventually you'll start shopping for a bigger boat. The size of your pocketbook determines your definition of "bigger"—the boat you want is always a little more expensive than the one you can really afford.

Shopping for a craft suitable for Lake Superior is more complicated than buying a new inland fishing rig. You need a boat that is seaworthy, roomy enough for fishing gear, and—in most instances—trailerable. Although many anglers choose to base at a marina during the fishing season, marina space on Superior is limited. A trailerable boat allows you to follow the fishing action or explore new waters.

As you begin to answer a few questions, you can narrow down your search for a new boat.

Most anglers agree that a serious Lake Superior fishing boat must have a V-hull and be *at least* eighteen or twenty feet in length. Boats of this size not only are seaworthy enough to reach the fishing grounds but will get you back to port if you are caught in a storm. However, the potential boat buyer can find any number of boats that meet these criteria. In order to choose the one that is best for you, ask yourself a few questions. Do you want a new or used boat? An inboard or outboard engine? A canvas top or a hard top? An aluminum

or a fiberglass hull? As you begin to answer these questions, you can narrow down your search for a new boat.

The type of boat you choose depends largely on your fishing style. If you are going to confine your fishing to nearshore trolling on nice days, an open boat will do. However, if you want to make overnight trips to Isle Royale or other distant destinations, you need a boat with a cabin and toilet facilities. Generally speaking, a boat with a covered bow and enclosed space serves best in the boating conditions you'll find on Lake Superior. When the lake is rough, waves frequently crash over the bow. If the bow is covered (a hard cover is much safer than canvas), you won't take on water. And an enclosed space provides warmth and shelter from the elements, an important consideration on a lake where you must often wear warm clothing even during the summer.

Learn From Charter Captains

Anyone planning to purchase a first Lake Superior rig should spend time on the water with a charter captain or another serious angler. Most love to talk about fishing and can give you lots of advice about what to look for when shopping for a new boat. No one knows the lake, boats, and fishing like those who are on the water every day. When scheduling the trip, explain that you want to learn about Lake Superior boats and fishing, so that the captain knows what to expect. You may even want to write down some questions you'd like to ask so that you don't forget about them when you are on the water.

Although the captain probably won't share *every* secret, you will get valuable opinions on boats and gear. Such advice is worth the price of a chartered trip. In fact, you may even want to pay a charter captain or another knowledgeable boater to accompany you and look over the boat you plan to purchase. The expense is certainly cheaper than buying the wrong boat.

The first decision you must make is whether to buy a new or used craft. If money isn't a problem, you can get exactly what you want when you buy new. However, trollers on a budget will have more latitude in the used market. When buying a used boat for the big lake, investigate the inland markets, too. Beware of craft from saltwater areas, because the corrosive effects of salt water can cause deterioration to the engine and the rest of the boat. When you buy any used boat, have it thoroughly checked out by a competent mechanic prior to your first fishing trip.

Should you get a fiberglass or aluminum hull? Boat owners can wax long on the virtues and drawbacks of each. Aluminum hulls are generally lighter, an advantage for trailering. Some complain that aluminum is noisy, although foam-filled hulls are not. Fiberglass-hulled boats tend to sit lower in the water and ride better.

Boat owners also have strong opinions about powering a craft. Most agree that a dual power source adds a measure of safety to a boat. Some choose twin outboards for this reason. Others run well-maintained inboards or stern drives. Just make sure your choice has adequate power for the boat. Most single-engine boats have small auxiliary motors, outboards used primarily for trolling. However, the trolling motor must have enough power to push the boat if your main engine breaks down. A high-thrust prop on your trolling motor can improve handling. If your trolling motor has an alternator, you can charge your batteries while you troll.

Personal preferences will guide your choices for the interior design of your boat. However, not all boats are made for fishing. You need a clear stern with room to fish, and sturdy gunwales on which to mount downriggers and rod holders. A

When buying a used boat, beware of craft from saltwater areas, because the corrosive effects of salt water can cause deterioration to the engine and the rest of the boat.

hard top is warmer and more durable than canvas, and has structural strength for mounting radar or other equipment. Make sure you have ample space for storing extra gear and fuel.

Required Equipment

Powerful and unpredictable, Lake Superior demands the respect of every boater and leaves little margin for error. You must have the proper equipment and know how to use it. On both U.S. and Canadian waters, laws require that certain safety equipment be carried on board your craft. Required equipment varies with the size of the craft, but it is your responsibility to know what you need before you head out. You can find out if your boat meets the requirements by contacting the United States Coast Guard or Canadian Coast Guard. If enforcement officers find you on the water without the necessary gear—and on-board inspections are not uncommon—they may ticket you and order you ashore.

On United States waters, the Coast Guard requires the following:

- **Personal flotation devices** (PFDs or life preservers) are required for each person on board. Regulations for the specific type required vary with the size of the craft, but all PFDs must be Coast Guard–approved, readily accessible, and in good condition.

- **Navigation lights** are required on any boat operated between sunset and sunrise. Requirements vary with the size of the boat.

- **Fire extinquishers** are required on motorboats under twenty-six feet with enclosed fuel or engine compartments or permanently installed fuel tanks. All motorboats over twenty-six feet must have the proper number of Coast Guard-approved fire extinquishers on board.

- Horns or whistles capable of producing a two-second blast audible for one-half mile are required on every motorboat sixteen feet or longer.

- Backfire flame arrestors are required for all inboard and stern-drive engines.

- Ventilator ducts are required on all motorboats with enclosed engine or fuel compartments. Regulations call for at least two ducts, but the location varies with boat type and length.

- Visual distress signals—flags, flares, or lights— are required day and night for all boats over sixteen feet, and for any watercraft operated at night. Requirements vary for the type and size of watercraft.

**On Canadian waters,
the following equipment is required:**

- Minimum equipment for boats up to 5.5 meters in length includes one appproved life jacket, PFD, or life-saving cushion for each person on board; two oars with rowlocks or two paddles; one hand-held bailer or manual pump; and some type of sound signalling device. A Class B-I fire

Be Bulletproof

You should approach your Lake Superior boat the same way a pilot looks at an airplane. Make sure everything is scrupulously maintained to minimize chances for trouble on the water. Have the spare parts and equipment on board to deal with potential problems. If your craft is dead on the water on an inland lake, you have a good chance that someone will happen by and tow you in—not so on lonely Lake Superior.

extinquisher is required if the vessel has an in-board motor, fixed fuel tank, or a heating or cooking appliance that burns liquid or gaseous fuel. Permanently fitted lights must comply with Canadian Coast Guard regulations.

- Vessels more than 5.5 meters and up to eight meters in length must carry one approved lifejacket or PFD for everyone on board; two oars with rowlocks or two paddles, or one anchor with fifteen meters minimum of chain, cable, or rope; one bailer or one manual pump; one Class B-I fire extinquisher if the vessel is power driven or has a cooking or heating appliance that burns liquid or gaseous fuel; some type of sound signalling device; an approved lifesaving cushion or a buoyant heaving line (recommended minimum length of fifteen meters) or a life buoy 508, 610, or 762 millimeters in diameter; and six approved distress flares, including three A, B, or C types and three A, B, C, or D types. Permanently fitted lights must comply with Canadian Coast Guard regulations.

- Boats more than eight meters and up to twelve meters in length must meet the same requirements for PFDs, fire extinquishers, and lights as vessels in the 5.5 to eight meter category. In addition, they must have an anchor with at least fifteen meters of chain, cable, or rope; one bailer and one manual bilge pump; a sound device that complies with Canadian Coast Guard regulations; an approved life buoy 610 or 762 millimeters in diameter; not less than fifteen meters of buoyant line; and twelve approved distress flares, including six A, B, or C types and six A, B, C, or D types.

- Vessels more than twelve meters and up to twenty meters in length must meet the same regulations as smaller vessels for PFDs, anchors, lights, and sound devices. Boats of this size also must have an efficient bilge pumping system; two Class B-II fire extinquishers, one of which is next to the sleeping cabin entrance and the other next to the machinery space entrance; an additional Class B-II fire extinquisher if the vessel is power driven or has a heating or cooking appliance that burns liquid or gaseous fuel; a manual or power fire pump so water can reach any part of the vessel or one Class B-II fire extinquisher; two buckets to extinquish fire; one fire axe; one approved buoy of 762 millimeters in diameter or two approved life buoys 610 millimeters in diameter; fifteen meters minimum of buoyant line; and twelve approved distress flares, including six A, B, or C types and six A, B, C, or D types.

Navigational Gear

Every Lake Superior boater must understand the basics of navigation and have the equipment onboard to properly navigate in a fog or after dark. Sign up for the inexpensive navigation and boating safety classes offered in many communities. There you can learn how to use a compass, charts, and other navigational aids. Inland boaters can get by without basic boating skills; Great Lakes boaters cannot.

Even day trippers and boaters traveling familiar waters always should have a compass and charts on board. Most trollers are also equipped with loran C or global positioning navigation aids, both of which not only can guide you back to port in a fog but also let you pinpoint offshore fishing areas. Loran C operates from a system of radio towers and can be affected by weather. The satellite-based global positioning system offers twenty-four-hour worldwide coverage. Charter captains and other serious boaters often install radar units for traveling at night or in the fog. A radar reflector, which makes you visible to other craft using radar, is a good idea, too.

Depthfinders

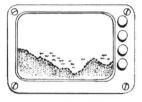

In-Dash Depthfinder

Think of your depthfinder as a navigational aid that also helps you find fish. A good rule of thumb when purchasing a new depthfinder is to purchase the best you can afford. The more expensive models have better definition, which helps you "read" what's going on beneath the boat. For Lake Superior, look for units that read depths to at least five-hundred feet.

Although depthfinders are relatively new on the angling scene, technological strides have been made in the past twenty years. The flasher units that first dominated the market are nearly obsolete. Some anglers still use them, although usually in conjunction with another unit. The same is true for paper graphs, once the hands-down choice for serious Lake Superior anglers. Although very accurate, paper graphs are expensive to operate because you must replace the rolls of paper. Now many anglers use their paper graphs as secondary units they can turn on when they want a better

Speed Is Relative

How precise should your fishing instruments be? Does it matter if your speed indicator shows you're trolling at 2.3 mph when you're actually going 2.7 mph? Not really, because instead of pinpoint accuracy you need a relative gauge of speed. What matters is that when your speed indicator says you're going 2.3 mph, you're catching fish. If you hear over the radio that someone is going 3.4 mph and really getting them, about all you know is that you should speed up. Don't be surprised if you find success at a slightly different speed. Remember, *their* speed indicator might be inaccurate, too.

view of what's going on down below. Current favorites are LCD and video units, both of which
have easy-to-read screens. LCDs are solid state with
no moving parts, while videos have a picture tube
similar to a television's.

A good depthfinder tells more than just the
depth. The better ones have zoom functions that
let you focus on a particular depth. Freeze and
memory functions let you study bottom structure
or "fishy" areas. Most units have temperature
probes that can give you surface water temperature readings. Some models are equipped with
speed indicators so you can judge your trolling
speed. In fact, a quality depthfinder with a temperature probe and speed indicator is about the
most useful piece of equipment a troller can acquire. Water temperature, depth, and trolling
speed—these three elements define trolling on the
Big Pond.

A quality depthfinder with a temperature probe and speed indicator is about the most useful piece of equipment a troller can acquire.

Communications

Fishing boats commonly carry two-way radios and
cellular phones. VHF-FM marine radios are preferred over citizen's band (CB) units, because they
have a longer range, are more reliable, can receive
official weather reports, and are continually moni-
tored by the Coast Guard and commercial vessels.
With a cellular phone, you can even call home
and say you'll be late for dinner. Portable AM radios let you check local weather reports.

For Safety's Sake

On Lake Superior, safe boating means being prepared for any situation that might arise. Having
spare quipment and a good tool kit on-board
means it's less likely you'll wind up dead in the
water ten miles offshore. Having plenty of on-
board storage space is important. You should

Be Prepared!

Safe boating involves carrying extra gear in case of emergency, including:

- a spare prop
- spark plugs
- hose clamps
- fuses
- electrical tape
- a spare battery
- a bilge pump
- ample fuel
- water-separator filter
- a first-aid kit

carry a spare prop, spark plugs, hose clamps, wire, fuses, and electrical tape to repair minor break-downs. Have at least one fully charged spare battery that is not being used. To prevent electrical malfunctions, be sure every power wire is properly fused.

Make sure your boat has a reliable bilge pump, and carry a portable or hand-operated bilge pump—and even sponges—for extra insurance. Always carry an ample supply of fuel. If going overnight, have the fuel capacity to reach your destination and, if necessary, return. Put a water-separator filter on the fuel line between the tank and the fuel pump. To prevent water from entering your fuel tanks, check the vent lines to see if they might take on water in rough seas. If you discover water in your fuel, get your tanks pumped immediately.

Even a minor cut can become a major problem if you do not have a first aid kit. A well-stocked kit contains items necessary for medical emergencies, as well as a flashlight, basic tools, disposable hand warmers, and even a pocket-sized first aid book. Spare clothing, rain gear, and PFDs add a measure of safety and comfort to your excursion.

Boating Basics

Boaters must understand their responsibilities and the "rules of the road" when operating in harbors and on the lake. Again, a little common sense can save a lot of trouble. Keep your distance from commercial craft and be careful when traveling in channels and shipping lanes. And, above all, keep an eye on the weather and stay sober.

Lake Superior is famous for its storms. Although the worst weather usually comes in November and March, ferocious storms can occur in any season. Always check the forecast before going out and monitor weather reports while you're on the water. Keep an eye to the sky, especially the south and west, because bad weather is most likely to come from those directions. Head for port before the storm arrives.

You also are likely to encounter dangerous fog on the lake, especially in June. On-the-water visibility may be reduced to zero, making it impossible to see or be seen. Unless you have excellent navigational equipment, stay on shore. Larger craft can use radar to keep track of nearby boats. Smaller craft should have a radar reflector on board so they'll appear on radar screens.

Navigational aids, such as lighted and unlighted buoys, are signposts for boaters. They may mark channels, nets, or scuba divers. At marinas and boat shows, you can often find small waterproof cards that identify various navigational aids. Generally, red and black companion buoys mark channels. Keep the red buoys to your starboard (right) side when heading toward shore or going upstream. Keep the black buoys to port (left). Stay between the red and black buoys. A black and white buoy marks the center of the channel. Stay close to the buoy and pass starboard.

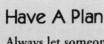

Have A Plan

Always let someone know where you are going and when you'll return, even if you plan to be out only for the afternoon. You can leave a short float plan with your name, the boat's number, a brief itinerary, and information about your radio (or lack of one) with the marina operator when you go out. Tell them who to call if your return is overdue. This simple exercise may save your life.

Dealing With Hypothermia

The constant cold is the greatest danger facing Lake Superior boaters. Being immersed in the water or merely getting wet can lead to the rapid onset of hypothermia, which is the lowering of your core body temperature. (Hypothermic victims are often described as suffering from exposure.) Because Superior's water is so cold, you can die from hypothermia on a sunny summer day. No matter the time of year, take the cold seriously.

Any victim exposed to cold air or water should receive hypothermia first aid. In some situations, rescuers may risk hypothermia, too. Mild cases, when the victim is alert, but shivering, and complains of numbness or pain from the cold, should be treated by keeping the victim warm. If possible, remove wet clothing and wrap the victim in a dry blanket. Exercise will generate heat. Give the victim warm, sweet drinks—not alcohol or coffee. Do the same for moderate cases, when the shivering may decrease or stop as the victim's core temperature cools further. However, do not give the victim warm fluids unless he or she is fully conscious, and limit exercise. Make sure a doctor examines the victim.

In severe cases of hypothermia, the victim may become confused or irrational, and may refuse help. This is a serious situation. Get the victim medical assistance as soon as possible. Be careful—rough handling of the victim (or a bumpy boat ride) can cause cardiac arrest. Treat as for shock by laying the victim down, elevating the feet, and covering with a dry blanket. Apply mild heat, such as disposable handwarmers, to the head, neck chest, and groin to prevent the body temperature from dropping further. Have another person also lie under the covers to warm the victim with body heat. Do not warm the victim with a hot shower.

Do not give a hypothermia victim warm fluids unless he or she is fully conscious, and limit exercise. Make sure a doctor examines the victim.

A critically hypothermic victim may appear dead. The victim may be unconscious, with cold, bluish-gray skin, and little or no pulse. Always assume the patient, who may be an apparent drowning victim, is revivable. Handle the victim very gently and tilt the head back to maintain an open airway. Check for breathing and a pulse for a full one or two minutes. If none is discernable, begin CPR immediately and continue until further help arrives or the victim revives.

If you fall into the lake, your survival time depends on a number of factors. Obviously, wearing a PFD is important, but the amount of clothing you have on (several layers are best) and your attitude also affect your chances. If others are in the water, huddle together to conserve warmth. Don't try to swim any further than very short distances, because experts estimate your potential swimming distance in very cold water as less than mile. If you can crawl up on the swamped boat or another floating object, you'll slow the onset of hypothermia.

The Temperature Game

RARELY, EXCEPT IN SHELTERED NEARSHORE AREAS, does Lake Superior's water warm up for comfortable swimming. Even in midsummer the waters stay frigid enough to make a polar bear shiver. The icy cold water affects trout and salmon activity. For that reason, the most essential piece of equipment that *any* Lake Superior angler can own is a simple thermometer or a temperature gauge. You must know the water temperature in order to plan your fishing strategy. Water temperature will determine how you fish, where you go, and what you use for bait. Think of water temperature as the "structure" you'll be fishing.

In the spring, water first absorbs the sun's warmth in shoreline shallows and areas protected by islands, near river mouths, or in places where red clay or other silts discolor the water. Because cold water is more dense, the warmer water "floats" on the surface. Early in the spring, this layer of warm water may be a few feet or less in thickness. Actively feeding fish will be right on the surface.

As the area of warm water grows larger, winds and currents cause sections to break loose and float offshore. You can find these offshore "plates" of warmer water by using a surface temperature gauge. Often a distinct *temperature break* forms where the warm and cold waters meet. Along this break the warm water cools and sinks. This causes drowned insects and other debris floating on the warmer water to collect along the break in what trollers call a *bug slick*. The warm water plates are shallowest near the surface temperature break and go to greater depths as you move toward the center. You might determine the depth of the subsurface break with a temperature probe or a sensitive depthfinder. Trollers often look for fish congregated along the surface and subsurface breaks.

In midsummer, surface water throughout the lake starts to warm up. If the weather is calm, temperature stratification can occur. However, because the lake is so cold and deep, a true thermocline never develops except in large bays and sheltered areas. On the open lake and areas with exposed coastline, winds and currents move the warm surface waters. The surface temperature might be 60 degrees one day and 42 the next. However, in shallow or protected areas, the warm water may extend to depths of seventy feet or more. Again, winds and currents cause water temperatures to fluctuate from one day to the next. As the days become shorter, the lake starts cooling down. Throughout

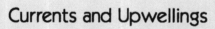

Currents and Upwellings

Summer water currents in Lake Superior generally move in a counterclockwise direction. Prevailing west winds combine with surface warming to create an easterly drift. This movement also causes upwellings of cold water along the western and northern shores. In some areas, such as off the tip of the Keweenaw Peninsula, the currents are strong enough to be visible. In fact, during the summer, currents entirely flush Chequamegon Bay about once every two weeks.

autumn, water temperatures decrease, until the lake is a very chilly 39 to 34 degrees.

The easiest way to locate temperature breaks is with a surface temperature gauge. However, look for visual clues such as bug slicks, changes in surface ripples, or even differences in water color. Sometimes you'll see gulls riding the break and feeding on insects collected in the slick. On calm days, you may even see surface-feeding trout and salmon. Once you find the break, use your surface temperature gauge to follow the edge, and start fishing.

If the water is very cold, active fish will be on the warm side of the break. However, because the edge of the temperature break is angular, the fish may not be right along the visible slick or edge. Troll in a zigzag pattern, following the break. Pay particular attention to your location relative to the break when you start catching fish. However, keep up the zigzag trolling even after you find the fish, because the irregular pattern produces more than does straight-line trolling. Also, be sure you troll in both directions along the break. Sometimes the fish strike only when you're trolling in a certain direction.

Mud lines are common phenomena off places like Duluth-Superior, where large rivers pour silty waters into the lake in the spring or after heavy rains. You can fish a mud line as you would a temperature break. Troll in zigzag patterns and remember that warm, muddy water may be floating over cold, clear water. Don't be afraid to troll right through the muddy water, because sometimes that's where the fish are.

Planer Boards

In spring and other times when the fish are very close to the surface, flatlines with stick baits or

In-line Planer

light spoons will produce. But if you troll flatlines directly behind the boat, three is a crowd. In fact, three trolled spoons will become a tangled mess. Even if you fish with longlines, you'll be dragging the lures through places you passed over with the boat. Many anglers believe surface-oriented fish spook away from boats.

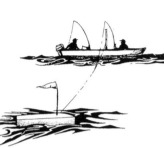

Planer Board

So on Lake Superior, where anglers can fish two or three lines apiece depending on local regulations, it pays to cover more water. For surface fishing, planer boards offer the most efficient option. A planer board is attached to a strong cord and planes away from the boat for fifty feet or more as you troll. You let your lures out behind the boat and then clip a small release to your fishing line. The release, which slides along the board line, is then allowed to slide out toward the planer board. When the release reaches the proper place along the board line, you close the bail on your reel and put the rod in a holder. You can fish two or more lines off each planer board and, with two boards, "cover the water" for some distance on either side of the boat. When a fish strikes, the line pulls free from the release so you can reel it in.

You can purchase planer board setups, although many anglers choose to make their own.

What's the Best Temperature?

If trout and salmon have their druthers, they seek out a preferred water temperature. Lake trout, for instance, prefer water at 49 to 50 degrees. Cohos and chinooks like water temperatures in the 53- to 55-degree range, while steelhead prefer a balmy 58 to 60 degrees. But on Lake Superior, you might be unable to find water that warm. In the spring, for example, look for the warmest water available. If you must fish cold water, slow down your presentations. Use bait and fish scents to trigger frigid fish.

You need a mast and small pulleys, a large reel to store the board line, and the boards, which are usually shaped from pine. Anyone who passed woodworking class in high school can make usable boards, and Lake Superior tackle shops sell components. To make your boards more visible to other boaters, paint them red or affix tiny orange flags.

Use medium-action rods eight to nine feet in length for planer board fishing. Quality spinning or level-wind reels should be spooled with 8- to 12-pound-test monofilament. Trolling places little stress on the rod, so you can get by with fairly light gear.

Fishing with trolling boards is easy. You can run your lures a short distance or over one-hundred feet behind the release. The outermost line should be the longest, so that you can play the fish without tangling the other lines. If you want the lures to ride a few feet beneath the surface, attach keel sinkers to your line. Be sure to make slow, wide turns when trolling with planer boards.

Some savvy anglers use boards to fish very shallow water without disturbing the fish. Let's say you find some lake trout holding on a shallow reef or along the shoreline. If you troll over them, they'll spook long before they see your

Release or Release?

Trollers *use* releases and *have* releases. When a fish strikes and pulls the line free from a planer board or downrigger release, trollers call the strike a release. Typical troller-speak might go something like this: "It was a good day. We had seven releases and caught five fish." Of course, a philosopher might contend that just going fishing is an act of release . . .

lures. Instead, run your boards over the shallow structure. This can be a very effective way to catch fish when they're hugging the shore. Also, if you see cohos or another species working the surface, try not to troll through the school. Instead troll alongside and let your board go over the fish.

Coho Working the Surface

Other Planing Devices

In recent years in-line planing devices have grown in popularity. These devices are set to pull your line away from the boat and then trip when a fish strikes. Most are lightweight and provide little interference when you fight the fish. In-line planers are inexpensive and easier to set up than boards. However, most models are difficult to fish in a heavy chop because the waves flip them over.

Some anglers use outrigger poles. These telescoping poles are affixed in holders. A line rigged on a pulley system runs the length of the pole. You attach your line to the release and then pull the line through the pulleys to carry the release to the end of the pole. Outrigger poles are handy if you fish alone or cannot mount a planer board mast on your boat. The drawback, however, is that you can only get your lure the distance of the outrigger pole away from your wake.

If It Smells Fishy . . .

Nature often leaves clues for the observant angler. Occasionally when you are trolling on Lake Superior—or fishing from shore—you'll catch a whiff of an intense fishy smell. Get ready, because you may soon have a strike. And always investigate when you see gulls or other birds concentrated in a particular area. They may lead you to a bug slick or a concentration of baitfish.

Divers

In-line divers fill the gap between planer boards and downriggers, allowing you to fish midrange depths and plane your lures away from the boat. Divers are an important weapon in the troller's arsenal, especially for fooling salmon. In fact, a common technique for cohos is to set a diver to run just behind the boat in the prop wash. In an apparent contradiction to the notion that cohos spook away from the boat, they seem attracted to engine turbulence. Why? Ask the fish.

Diver

You can buy divers in fluorescent or reflective fish-attracting colors. Divers are tied to your main line and the lure is run behind on a short leader. When a fish strikes, it trips the diver. Since divers pull hard when you troll, use stout tackle and strong line. You can also buy rubber snubbers to attach to your line to absorb the shock of a strike. The depth at which the diver will run depends on the size and weight of the device and the amount of line you release. Some divers can be set to plane away from the boat. Rods used for trolling with divers should be seven to eight feet long, with a firm action.

Early Risers Get Chinooks

Most trollers agree that chinook salmon are the toughest fish to catch in Lake Superior. Although charter captains and other trollers target them in some areas, most often the big salmon are an incidental catch. One reason is that most trollers are in the right place at the wrong time. Chinooks are extraordinarily light-sensitive, often sulking and refusing to strike during daylight hours. The best time to catch them is very early in the morning, around dawn, before sunlight penetrates the water. Savvy chinook anglers are often headed back to the dock when most anglers are starting their day.

Herring Dodger

Alluring Lures

Long, slender stick baits, both jointed and un-jointed models, are frequently used for early season surface trolling when the game fish are feeding on smelt. Be sure to troll slowly, say 1.5 to 2.5 mph., to allow the stick baits to run true. Dodger and fly combinations, perhaps with the added attraction of cut or live bait, are also effective. Try running a dodger and fly just behind the boat on a shallow downrigger. Later, when the water temperatures warm up, try trolling lightweight or flutter spoons.

Trolling Finesse

The difference between a nice day on the water and fish for supper might be as simple as varying your trolling speed. Charter captains and other experienced trollers try different speeds until they start catching fish. Sometimes, a short, quick burst of speed will trigger strikes. At other times, such as early spring when the water is cold, the slower you troll the better.

Some species, such as coho, prefer slightly faster trolling speeds. If you are hunting for salmon and catch one, make a few circles through the area to see if you find a school. Occasionally, you'll mark fish on your graph that are holding at a specific depth. Experiment with different lures, colors, and trolling speeds to see if you can get them to bite. If not, continue searching for active fish.

Deepwater Fishing

THE EXTREME DEPTH OF LAKE SUPERIOR boggles the minds of most inland anglers. On Minnesota's North Shore, for instance, you can find depths over two hundred feet within a mile of shore. Understandably, the fish you seek, especially lake trout, may be one-hundred feet or more beneath the surface. And you may have to troll at depths ranging from twenty to eighty feet to find the "surface-oriented" species such as coho salmon.

Fishing deep water presents a special challenge to the sport angler. You need enough weight to bring your lure to the depth where the fish are located, yet you want to use tackle light enough so you can play the fish. In the old days, trollers used stout tackle with braided copper line and heavy lead weights or trolling plates that pulled their spoons into the depths where monster lake trout lurked. The method was crude, perhaps, but effective. And a thirty-pound lake trout can make a good account of itself even with a one-pound sinker hanging from its jaw.

Because of Superior's tremendous depths, the fish you seek—especially lake trout—may be one-hundred feet or more beneath the surface.

Downrigger Basics

In the old days, the weights deepwater anglers used occasionally outweighed the fish that they caught.

Downrigger

The heavy tackle necessary to handle all that weight diminished the fight of even big fish.

Downriggers revolutionized deepwater fishing, making it possible to fish the depths with relatively light tackle. Better still, downriggers allow trollers to be versatile and present their lures at several depths when searching for active fish.

The downrigger is a transom-mounted winch and boom with a large weight attached to a heavy cable. The fishing line is attached to a clip device called a release, and the rod is placed in an attached holder. The lure trails behind the downrigger apparatus. When a fish strikes, the fishing line is pulled free from the release, so that you fight the fish unencumbered by the weight. After you land the fish, you reel up the downrigger weight and reset your line in the release.

Downriggers fall into two basic categories: hand-cranked and electric. Both have their advantages. Hand-cranked winches are less expensive and well suited to smaller boats. You can also quickly reel up the weight if the bottom suddenly becomes shallower. Electric winches save on elbow grease—an important consideration if you are fishing with two to four downriggers.

When choosing downriggers, be sure the boom is long enough to keep the cable out of your props.

Most downriggers have a clutch drag that allows cable to pull out if the weight catches on an obstruction. A counter shows you how much cable you have let out so you can determine the approximate depth that you are fishing. Booms come in short and long lengths. Typically, short booms are used with downriggers set up on the stern and longer ones off the sides. When choosing downriggers, be sure the boom is long enough to keep the cable out of your props. Some downriggers are equipped with coaxial cable and subsurface temperature gauges so you can monitor the water temperatures down below.

Downriggers are subject to lots of stress, especially when you are fishing deep or hang up on the bottom. Some unlucky anglers have had the downriggers torn off their boats. Be sure to use backing plates when you mount them.

On Bombs

Anglers often call the heavy lead weights attached to the downrigger cable "bombs." Depending on the depth you plan to fish and the size of your downrigger, bombs can range in weight from three pounds to twelve or more pounds. However, eight- and ten-pounders are most commonly used. You can buy molds to cast your own bombs or purchase them at tackle stores.

Bombs come in several different styles. Some are just round "cannonballs" with a ring to attach the cable. Other balls have a flat rudder for better tracking behind the boat. Those that track the best are fish-shaped. Each has a different use. Balls are best for bouncing bottom, because they generally don't hang up. If they do, often you can pull them free just by backing up the boat. If you don't "fish dangerously" by bouncing bottom or trolling close to reefs and other structures, fish-shaped weights make the best choice. Although many bombs are unpainted, others have fluorescent paint or rubberized coatings. Some even offer the extra fish-attracting flash of prism tape. You can also buy bombs that have special compartments for fish scents.

"Bombs"

Releases

The release is the device attaching your line to the downrigger. The release may be located at the weight or anywhere along the downrigger cable.

By using two or more releases on a downrigger you can "stack" your lines at various depths. Release designs vary from simple rubber band setups to spring-loaded devices. The model you choose depends on your fishing style, although adjustable-tension releases are the most versatile. Choose designs that minimize stress and wear on your fishing line. You can attach your release to a Plexiglas fin that rides above the bomb. The fin will swivel in the direction that you troll, so the lure runs true.

You can run your lures at various distances behind the release. The distance depends on the type of lure and the fishing situation. If you think the fish are spooked by the passing boat, run your lures further back. However, the greater the distance between the release and the lure, the more line drop—the interval in which the line is slack between the moment the fish strikes, breaking the line free from the release, and the time the line becomes taut with the rod.

Stacking is a method for running two or more lines on one downrigger. Releases are staggered at various depths along the cable (don't exceed the legal number of lines). Some trollers use a short "cheater" or "slider" line that slides along the trolling line on a snap swivel. The cheater rides halfway between the surface and the release. However, when you get a strike on the cheater the snap swivel must slide down the main line until stopped by the terminal rigging before you can set the hook.

Rods and Reels

Downrigger fishing rods must be long and limber and have a medium action, because the rod is bowed over when the line is set in the release. Preferred lengths are from seven to nine feet. Many trollers favor Fiberglas and graphite/glass composites. You can use graphite, but some of the new

If you think the fish are spooked by the passing boat, run your lures further back.

high-density graphite rods might shatter from the
constant strain.

A large-capacity spinning reel or a free-spool-
ing level-wind with a star drag works best. Most
anglers spool up with twelve- to fifteen-pound-
test monofilament. Stiff, abrasion-resistant mono
is preferred. Don't use line that is too heavy, because it diminishes lure action. You can handle
anything that swims in Lake Superior with fifteen-
pound-test.

Dodgers and Flashers

Dodgers and flashers are in-line fish attractors
commonly used with downriggers. Both resemble
an oversized spoon without a hook. The difference between them is in the action: a dodger has a
side-to-side action, and a flasher rotates. Each style
gives off different flash and vibration patterns.
Both impart additional action to the lure.

Herring Dodger

Dodgers and flashers generally are run about
four to six feet behind a heavy weight so that the
attractor works properly. The lure, which may be
a fly, plastic squid, plug, or spoon, is attached to a
short monofilament leader. The shorter the leader,
the more action in the lure, especially with flies
and squids. Leaders for dodgers average twelve to
thirty inches, while those for flashers run eighteen to thirty inches. You should tie up your leader
rigs before going fishing, to save time. Tip your
lure with cut bait for more attraction. Another
trick is to run just a flasher behind your cannonball and put a lure on a stacked line above it.

Bouncing Bottom

Bouncing bottom—literally—with the downrigger ball is a favorite lake trout trolling technique anywhere anglers can get away with it. You
must have a smooth, obstruction-free bottom to

avoid hang-ups. If the bottom is uneven, run your cannonballs as close as you dare. The object of bouncing bottom is to put your lure right where the lake trout are holding. The cannonball makes noise and stirs up sediments as it bounces along, attracting fish, which then strike the lure.

Most bottom bouncers prefer flutter spoons because of their enticing action. However, don't be afraid to try stick baits or meat. For colors, try silver, black, purple, and luminescent. Run the lure a short distance behind the ball. However, if you see fish on your locator and they seem unwilling to strike, try running the lures further behind the ball. In some situations the cannonball seems to spook the fish.

You can hang up in areas where the bottom seems flat as a pancake. Snagging a downrigger is often more exciting than catching fish. It's as if a big hand has just risen out of the water and grabbed your transom. Throw the boat in neutral and reel in the lines and other downriggers as fast as you can. If you can, try to back up and pull the bomb free. If it is truly stuck, you'll have no choice but to cut or break the cable. You can lower the

Can You Release Them?

Will a deepwater lake trout survive if it is released? Yes, say both charter captains and fish biologists, provided you play the fish carefully, handle it gently, and let it go quickly. Lake trout undergo a pressure change when you bring them up from the depths. If you play the fish, rather than winch it to the surface, it has time to adjust to the change. Net the fish, then carefully hold it while you remove the hook. Don't hold the fish by the eyes or the gills, or allow it to thrash on the deck. Treat the trout as though someone promised to pay you a million bucks if it was still alive a week after you released it.

odds of becoming hung up by using cannonballs. Some anglers drop a smaller "tickler" weight below the bomb on a lighter line, a concept similar to the dropper system for sinkers used by stream anglers. A few tricky anglers use a length of heavy chain instead of a ball. The chain drags across an uneven bottom and rattles with fish-attracting noise. As for trolling speeds, as slow as possible is the general rule.

What Depth?

Many anglers use the bouncing bottom technique only when nothing else is working, because it is hard on equipment. More often, you'll use a downrigger to present your baits at midrange depths. However, finding the right depth to fish requires some guesswork and experimentation. You must figure out at what depth the active fish are holding and what lures will fool them.

Siwash Hook

Start your search for fish at the dock. Try to pick the brains of other anglers for current info. Find out where they have been and how they caught fish. Then you have a starting point. When you get on the water, consider all possible factors.

If the hook is difficult to remove, you can cut it off with a sidecutter. Sometimes lake trout are bloated or bug-eyed from the pressure change. Stroke the belly to deflate the swim bladder. *Do not* puncture the swim bladder with a needle prior to release. Once the fish returns to the water its swim bladder will readjust to the pressure as it goes back to the depths.

Anglers who frequently release lake trout and other fish often replace the treble hooks on their spoons with single Siwash-style hooks. These hooks remove from the fish easier, don't become tangled in the net, and also hook more fish. On some lures with two or more treble hooks, you can remove the forward and middle hooks without impairing the action

Is it cloudy or sunny? Is the water temperature stable? Do the fishing boats seem to be heading in one direction or are they spread out?

Think about what sort of baitfish might be in the area. Smelt are diurnal, which means they come in to shallow water at night and retreat to deeper water in the day. Herring might be miles offshore. Usually smelt school tightly, while herring may be more scattered. Keep watching your depthfinder for schools of baitfish.

When you start fishing, run some standard lures at various depths. You can stack lines on your downriggers and run divers, too. If you don't catch anything, start changing colors, lure styles, and depths until you strike a winning combination. Even if you start catching fish, continue experimenting with one or two lines. The fish may go deeper as the sun climbs higher, or turn off for some other reason. It pays to keep your options open.

A New Frontier?

Commercial fishermen say herring are currently more abundant than they have been in decades. Biologists have also found that lake trout now eat more herring. Some anglers believe this change in diet from smelt to herring will lead to changes in fishing strategies. Herring schools roam the entire lake. They prefer cold water and can reach great depths. Predator fish feeding on these schools may be out of reach of the average troller who is fishing temperature breaks, mudlines, and near shore areas.

Herring have the potential to significantly alter lake trout behavior. Since they prefer cold water, herring move offshore about the time trollers begin fishing in the spring. Some biologists say that herring and lake trout may move near shore during the cold winter months instead, when few anglers look for them. Some charter captains speculate that a new frontier for trollers lies five miles or further offshore, where herring schools spend the summer months. In order to be successful in a new location, you must find currents that influence fish movements. To find these currents, ask commercial fishermen where they have found herring. Sometimes you may see the floats that mark their herring nets when you are fishing offshore. As far as fishing techniques, you're on your own. This is a new frontier: experiment and explore.

Old-timers' Tricks

ALTHOUGH THE ADVENT of downriggers and planer boards marked the beginning of a new era for Lake Superior fishing, these tackle advances did not render techniques the old-timers used obsolete. For instance, in the Upper Peninsula many lake trout anglers don't carry a fishing rod. Instead they have a short, wooden bobbing stick wrapped with strong Dacron line. On most days, the effectiveness of bobbing puts modern techinques to shame. The same is true of other old-timers' tricks.

Doing The Jig

Lake trout are suckers for the quick lift and flutter-down action of a well-fished jig, especially if it is tipped with some cut or live bait. However, you can spend a long time fishing on Lake Superior and never see anyone using a jig. Why? Because everyone is too busy trolling or casting to give jigs a try. However, if you find a concentration of lake trout, jigging is undoubtedly the best way to fish for them. And you can use light spinning tackle to fish depths of fifty feet or more.

    However, the jigging technique for lake trout is somewhat different from the typical drag-and-twitch that most anglers use for walleyes. When

Bobbing Stick

Marabou Jig

jigging for lake trout, use a sharp, forceful action that causes the lure to hop up from the bottom and then flutter down. Most often, lake trout strike on the downstroke.

The size and style of jig to use depends on where you're fishing. A shore-caster working the edge of a river current might get by with a one-quarter-ounce marabou crappie jig, while an angler working a deep reef off Isle Royale needs a bucktail jig weighing a half ounce or more. Use a jig heavy enough to readily sink to the depth of the fish. If you must contend with wind, waves, or current, you may need to use a heavier jig to maintain control.

Generally, white and fluorescent green seem to be the most productive jig colors. You can use unadorned jigs or those dressed with bucktail, marabou, or plastic twister tails. Adding bait or fish-attracting scents will make your jig more appealing. Good baits to use include strips of sucker meat or lake herring and smelt. Anglers often cut strip baits into long, slender shapes with forked tails to more closely resemble bait fish. Adding a trailing stinger hook to your jig helps keep the strip meat from pulling free and nabs short-striking trout.

Bobbing

Technology has changed bobbing over the years. Even bobbing sticks, also called gebbus or debbies on the U.P., are now made of plastic, although traditionalists still opt for wooden models.

Actually, there's nothing to bobbing. Just grab your gebbu and practice your stroke. Pretty soon you'll be bobbing with the best of 'em. Bobbing is a deep-water vertical jigging technique handed down through generations of Scandinavian anglers. Among the Finns of the Upper Peninsula it is still a popular lake trout fishing method both summer and winter.

Technology has changed bobbing over the years. One no longer needs strong legs and a keen understanding of shoreline landmarks in order to

walk out on the ice and find the best winter bobbing spots. Snowmobiles, ATVs, and fish-finders
are now available. Bobbing tackle has changed,
too. Wire or Dacron lines have replaced the tarred
cotton or linen lines used in the past. Even bobbing sticks, also called gebbus or debbies on the
U.P., are now made of plastic, although traditionalists still opt for wooden models.

Bobbers generally fish in water ranging from
one-hundred to over two-hundred feet deep. The
bobber keeps about three-hundred feet of wire line
wrapped around the stick, which holds about two
feet of line for each complete turn. At the end of
the line is a crimped swivel, to which is attached a
ten- or twenty-foot monofilament leader. A heavy
jig is tied to the leader. In the U.P., the saltwater
barracuda jig is a favorite, but you can find several styles of bobbing jigs in tackle shops near Lake
Superior. Most are manufactured locally.

The jig is invariably tipped with cut bait. Smelt
are most commonly used in the U.P., although
anglers fish with whitefish bellies, which are
tougher, when they can get them. Herring, cisco,
or sucker, if available, could be used. Making the
proper slices when cutting bait is angling alchemy.
Some prefer smelt heads, others the tail. Slice them
as you choose. Just remember to keep the skin
facing upward when on the jig. The flash from
the skin and scales adds to the bait's appeal.

Smelt

One does not become a master bobber the first
time out. Learning the proper bobbing stroke, like
playing the violin, requires practice. You want the
jig far below you to swim in a natural, fish-entic-
ing manner. You can jig with the bobbing stick or
by holding the line. However, connecting with a
monster lake trout or stray chinook while holding wire line in your fingers could be very painful.

Because wire and Dacron lines do not stretch,

you can feel fish strike and set the hook. Then the fun begins. Somehow, you must coax an unwilling lake trout off the bottom, keep over one hundred feet of line from becoming tangled, and avoid spilling your coffee while confined inside a portable ice-fishing shelter. Who said ice-fishing is boring?

In many areas, bobbers travel three or four miles offshore to reach the fishing grounds. Nearly everyone uses a teepee as an ice-fishing shelter. This low-profile shelter can withstand the ever-present winter winds. Although the temperatures outside might be below zero, inside the teepee a bobber can use a small heater to stay warm and even cook lunch.

Ice-fishing Teepee

In the summer, anglers from the U.P. bob for lake trout off Isle Royale. They use anchors with three hundred feet or more of rope in order to hold the boat in position over deepwater structure. The technique is the same as when winter fishing—and the weather is slightly warmer.

Skis

Out around the Apostle Islands and off the coast of the western U.P., some trollers use devices called skis to fish for lake trout on the bottom. The ski is similar to a sinking planer board. It is attached to the boat with a running line, and then a lead weight is hung beneath the ski. Baits are run from leaders at various points between the weight and the ski. When used in the old-fashioned way, the entire setup must be pulled in to land a fish. The ski may be brought in with a large reel or pulled hand over hand.

Wire-Line Fishing

Using braided or single-strand wire instead of fishing line is a new-old bottom-bouncing technique.

You might say the old-timers would have done it this way if the tackle had been available. Some wire-line trollers swear the method consistently outproduces downrigging.

Stout rods as long as nine feet with roller guides (converted muskie rods work well) and level-wind reels with star drags are necessary gear. Spool some Dacron backing on the reel and then wind on up to one-thousand feet of wire. Terminal tackle begins with a swivel attached to the wire, followed by a rubber snubber. A one-pound snag-proof weight is attached to the swivel. Lures are run on a six- to twenty-foot monofilament leader.

Let out line until you can feel the weight ticking along the bottom. Physical fitness is required. You must hold on to the rod and continuously pump it to get the proper lure action—just like the old-timers used to do. Because wire line has no give, strikes are jolting and you'll feel every tug in the fight.

Cowbells

Trolling with cowbells is like pulling a hardware store behind the boat. Nevertheless, these multiple-spinner rigs are effective trout-getters, especially when the water is cold. To fish with cowbells you need stout tackle, such as a trolling rod and level-wind reel spooled with low-stretch Dacron. Use a monofilament leader of at least ten-pound-test ahead of the cowbells. Behind the cowbell run an eighteen-inch leader to the bait. Sucker minnows and dead smelt are good choices.

Cowbells

From Pike to Panfish

SOME ANGLERS ARE JUST LEECHERS. They're not pan-handlers or parasites, they just like walleyes. After all, the walleye reigns supreme on the inland lakes of the Lake Superior region. On the Big Pond, however, fishable populations occur only in estuaries and relatively shallow areas. But in these places you can find terrific action for everything from large sport fish like northern pike, walleyes, and smallmouth bass to various panfish, including yellow perch, crappies, and menominees.

In fact, the old adage about big waters producing big fish certainly holds true here. The average walleye, northern, and smallmouth is heftier than its inland relatives. And trophy-sized specimens are a distinct possibility. However, these are fragile fisheries, because it takes many years for a fish to grow to trophy size in Superior's cold waters. Shortsighted anglers have already damaged some populations by keeping all the big ones. Fortunately, fishing regulations are beginning to incorporate size limits and reduced bags in an effort to improve the quality of fishing. But it is still up to individual anglers to show respect for these wonderful resources. Be a conservationist. Practice catch-and-release.

The old adage about big waters producing big fish certainly holds true here. The average walleye, northern, and smallmouth is heftier than its inland relatives.

Walleyes

Walleye

Nearly every large river that's too warm to be a trout stream has resident walleyes. These fish spawn and live in the river, although a portion of the population may venture out into Lake Superior to feed. Walleyes from the St. Louis River, for instance, leave the river estuary during the summer and head east along the South Shore, where trollers frequently catch them.

The best time to fish for river walleyes is spring and early summer. When the season opens they'll be concentrated near spawning areas. At this time it is not unusual to catch spawn-heavy walleye hens weighing ten pounds or more. Following the spawn, the population will spread out and begin feeding in earnest. Often you'll find river walleyes in surprisingly shallow water, because the dark or turbid water in these streams transmits very little light. Usually, they'll be in the main channel or in areas with moderate currents.

Minnows and nightcrawlers are good baits, especially when trolled on a spinner rig. However, crankbaits and even Lake Superior trolling lures account for their share of walleyes. If you fish from shore or an anchored boat, it's hard to beat a plain jig tipped with bait.

You can fish for open-water walleyes in several locations. Anglers have discovered that the walleyes that spawn in the St. Louis River migrate to the open lake during the summer and then move eastward along the South Shore. Often they suspend fifteen feet or more beneath the surface. Trollers use shallow-diving stickbaits off planer boards or spoons and divers to reach the fish. If the walleyes are deep, they can be taken by downrigging. However, Charter captains fish walleyes in the Duluth-Superior harbor whenever the lake is too rough for trolling.

At Chequamegon Bay near Ashland and Huron Bay east of L'Anse, most walleye fishing occurs in the spring and early summer. In Chequamegon, try Kakagon Slough or the main channels of the bay. Depending on the season, walleyes might be anywhere from three to forty feet deep. You can locate them by trolling or drifting. On Huron Bay, anglers catch walleyes from mid-May until July. Then the fish disappear. The Huron Bay walleye fishery is still developing and anglers have not figured out late summer patterns. Most likely, the walleyes move out into the main lake.

A number of Ontario rivers support walleyes, although they are fished mostly by locals. Some rivers have resident walleye populations, but in other, generally smaller, streams the walleyes spawn in the river during the spring and migrate back to the lake. Although the fishing may not compare with a fly-in camp, and access to some rivers is difficult, you can catch some nice fish. A few Ontario rivers that merit a second look include the Pigeon, Pine, Kaministiquia, Black Sturgeon, Prairie, Pic, and Michipicoten.

Northern Pike

In 1659, the French explorer Pierre Esprit Radisson reported taking "sturgeons of vast bigness, and Pycks seven feet long" from a channel in Chequamegon Bay. Perhaps, like so many anglers, Radisson stretched the truth, although undoubtedly Lake Superior was then home to some enormous northern pike. It still is. From the bustling harbor of Duluth-Superior to the wilderness bays of Isle Royale, you can still find pike as long as your leg.

Northern Pike

In recent years inland anglers have learned that pike prefer cold water and that they seek cool depths to prey on high-protein forage species such as cisco. Perhaps this is why pike do so well in certain areas on Lake Superior. If you can find places where pike have access to the weedy shallows they require for spawning, you'll find large northerns lurking in the vicinity.

How do you catch them? In the spring you can cast with spoons, spinnerbaits, large jigs, or muskie baits in shallow areas where pike spawn or along channel edges. More than a few Lake Superior springtime pike have been fooled with dead smelt fished on the bottom. Also, look for northerns lurking near schools of spawning suckers. Try the deep water with a slow current close to the spawning area. In the summer, try trolling in deeper water. Don't be surprised if summertime northerns prove difficult to catch. As autumn approaches, look for fishing action to pick up. Then you'll see the old-timers still-fishing with bobbers and live suckers near springs or mouths of cold tributaries feeding into harbors or bays.

If anglers want to catch trophy pike, then they must practice catch-and-release. Unfortunately, popular pike-fishing spots like Chequamegon and Huron Bays are producing few trophy fish these days because fishing pressure removed the big northerns from the population. However, pike ten pounds or more still turn up. In Marquette, anglers look for pike in the lower harbor and near the ore docks. Pike fishing was better when the power plant discharged warm water in the harbor. Now the discharge is offshore.

Occasionally, northern pike show up where you least expect them. Sometimes they swim down from inland lakes along tributary streams and grow fat in estuary areas or near river mouths. More than one angler has been surprised when a pike hammered a spoon intended for trout or salmon. In Ontario, the sheltered waters of Black, Nipigon,

> Occasionally, northern pike show up where you least expect them. Sometimes they swim down from inland lakes along tributary streams and grow fat in estuary areas or near river mouths.

and Batchawana Bays all harbor pike. Some of these places are lightly fished.

Smallmouth Bass

Those who know Chequamegon Bay say it has one of the world's best smallmouth bass fisheries. Sure, locals always say nice things about their home waters, but on Chequamegon the proof is in the pudding. Just a decade ago anglers could expect to catch smallmouth over five pounds during the course of an average day of fishing. However, excessive harvest of big bass by unscrupulous anglers has reduced the average size of the fish. Wisconsin is expected to enact restrictive harvest regulations to restore quality to the fishery. Some say Chequamegon Bay has the potential to produce smallmouth weighing eight pounds or more.

Smallmouth Bass

Since Chequamegon is the primary smallmouth bass fishery on the lake—although they are also found in Ontario's Batchawana Bay—let's talk specifically about how to catch them there. Think of the bay as a large, deep inland lake although the bay offers little of the rocky structure considered typical smallmouth bass habitat. Bass fishing begins in May, as water temperatures climb to 65 degrees, and the best time to catch trophy smallmouth is during May and June.

Fly-rodding for Chequamegon smallmouth is popular with those who are in the know. Fly-casters recommend matching a weight-forward bass taper fly line with 5- to 7-weight fly rods. The bass are not leader-shy, so you can use heavy 1X leaders. Favorite subsurface patterns include the Wooly Bugger and the Clouser Minnow. Surface fishing is very good. Use hard-bodied cork poppers because the fish tend to swallow hair-bodied popping bugs. Those using spinning tackle should fish with jigs, preferably with barbless single hooks

Cork Popper

to facilitate easy release of the fish. Tipping your jig with bait usually isn't necessary.

Ontario's Batchawana Bay is also noted for its fine smallmouth fishery, producing bass up to five pounds. The best place to fish for them is among the tiny "flowerpot" islands near Batchawana Island, which shelters the bay from the main lake. The flower pots are also home to colonies of nesting blue herons. This is classic smallmouth fishing. You can anchor off shoals and cast with jigs or other proven bass baits. Expect smallies weighing two to three pounds.

The best place to fish for smallmouth bass is among the tiny "flowerpot" islands near Batchawana Island, which shelters the bay from the main lake.

Two other places that merit smallmouth bass anglers' investigation are the St. Louis River at Duluth-Superior and the Kaministiquia River at Thunder Bay. Both have healthy, lightly fished smallmouth populations. Although the river bass will be smaller than those in Chequamegon Bay, you can find fast action. However, release your fish to preserve the quality of these fisheries.

Panfish

You can find crappies in the St. Louis River estuary, and yellow perch there and in other shallow areas. However, perch fishing in Chequamegon Bay and Whitefish Bay has declined. Good perch populations exist in Batchawana Bay. The crappies in the St. Louis River are sizable and lightly fished. Another locally popular panfish are menominees, which can be caught near river mouths in the spring, using tiny hooks baited with a salmon egg or piece of earthworm.

Ice Fishing

IT TAKES AN EXCEPTIONALLY COLD WINTER for Lake Superior to become completely covered with ice. Freeze-up for inland waters arrives in November, but the big lake resists winter's onslaught for months. Large, sheltered areas such as Chequamegon Bay and Thunder Bay usually have ice that is safe to walk on around the first of the year. The main lake may not begin making ice until late February, usually when the weather is cold and calm.

The ice floes move with the winds and the currents. Even a slight shift of wind can cause this pack ice to break away from shore or to develop cracks called leads. Both situations pose extreme danger for anglers. On several occasions stranded anglers have had to be rescued on the ice.

You must use extreme caution whenever you venture out on a frozen Lake Superior. Always carry a spud to check the ice ahead of you, because the ice can vary in thickness. In the U.P., they talk about one poke, two poke, and three poke ice, referring to how many times you can hit it with a spud before you break through. Be sure someone knows exactly where you are going and when you plan to return. Those who travel off-shore to bob for lake trout often drag a small boat

You must use extreme caution whenever you venture out on a frozen Lake Superior.

along as extra insurance. Carrying a compass is also a good idea because snow or fog can reduce visibility to a whiteout. If the conditions look risky, stay on shore. The best way to learn about Lake Superior ice-fishing is to accompany experienced anglers. They can teach you how to read the conditions and show you how to fish. Don't be afraid to give ice-fishing on the big lake a try, because it can be exciting and very rewarding.

Chequamegon's Bounty

As soon as Wisconsin's Chequamegon Bay has a safe coating of ice, anglers start fishing for splake. These lake trout/brook trout hybrids are eager winter biters that average from two to five pounds. In addition, you can also ice-fish for brown trout, lake trout, and other species, including an occasional sturgeon.

Ice-fishing usually starts in January, when safe ice forms in the bay. Look for the fish to hold in water from twelve to forty feet deep. Popular fishing spots include the Washburn Coal Dock and the mouths of the Sioux and Onion rivers. As winter progresses, the fish move to deeper water, and the splake action tapers off. As ice conditions improve, anglers go farther from shore to bob for lake trout in 70 to 120 feet of water.

When the splake are biting, they're fairly easy to catch. Emerald shiners, suspended from a tip-up or attached to a jig, are a favorite bait. Lively minnows seem to work the best. Fish near the bottom, but also experiment at other depths. Sometimes browns, cohos, and other fish cruise just beneath the ice.

Early winter is a good time to fish for perch and walleyes. Again, success tapers off in midwinter. However, when the ice begins to deteriorate in late winter, perch and walleyes start biting again.

Splake, lake trout/brook trout hybrids, are eager winter biters that average from two to five pounds.

Cohos, herring, and whitefish appear in the catch, too. If you're looking for something different, try ice-fishing for smelt with your bluegill gear. On a good day you'll catch fifty or more of the silver scrappers, enough to cook for a meal or to freeze as bait.

Love Those 'Loopers

Sometimes it seems that half of Duluth's population is standing on the ice off French River, fishing for Kamloops rainbow trout. 'Loopers, as these chunky rainbows are affectionately known, hang around the shoreline in growing numbers throughout the winter as they stage for their spring spawning run. By February, when the lake freezes over in a typical year, nearshore waters are lousy with 'loopers. It is not uncommon to see several dozen or more big rainbows on a typical morning outing.

How can you see fish beneath the ice? Well, that's part of the thrill of 'looper fishing. Anglers typically set up a portable ice-fishing tent over waters that are less than six feet deep. You can then watch fish swim in to investigate your bait—or just ignore it as they go past. Because the water is so clear and shallow, ultralight tackle is the rule. The best anglers land trout averaging three to eight pounds with 2-pound-test line.

Tiny marabou jigs, readily available at Duluth area tackle shops, have led to the demise of many a 'looper. Black and purple are favorite colors. You can tip the jigs with maggots or wax worms. Actually just about any small lure or bait will catch fish, because Kamloops—at least by Lake Superior standards—are obliging biters.

Looper Jig

If you travel any distance to fish for 'loopers, bring both ice-fishing tackle and spinning gear. Strong winds can push the ice pack away from

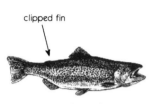

clipped fin

"Clipped"
Rainbow Trout

Look For Clips

All rainbow trout
stocked in Lake
Superior are marked
with fin clips so they
can be identified as
hatchery fish. In some
places, such as
Minnesota, bag limits
differ for wild
steelhead and
stocked rainbow
trout. Be sure you've
properly identified
your catch before
you keep it.

shore. Openwater anglers employ the same light-line, small-baits approach. Try fishing the same jig beneath a float.

Near Duluth, ice-fishing is so popular that places like French River become crowded. Stay away from the crowd if you can. The noise and activity spook the fish.

From March until ice-out, you can find steelhead and other fish staging to spawn in the vicinity of any river mouth. The fish are most likely to be active and in shallow water early in the morning.

Wild For Whitefish

In some bays, especially in Michigan and Ontario, anglers have learned how to catch lake whitefish through the ice. Lake whitefish are strong fighters that are very good to eat when cooked fresh or smoked. Jigging spoons and small minnows produce consistently. In Michigan, anglers use salmon eggs, canned corn, and steelhead eggs (boiled so they'll harden and stay on the hook) for bait. Often anglers first chum an area, using a weighted can suspended on a line to bring the chum to the bottom. Although lake whitefish may weigh five pounds or more, light lines are preferred.

In some locations, anglers have discovered they can catch herring through the ice. In Minnesota, the Duluth area and Burlington Bay at Two Harbors are locally popular spots to ice-fish for herring. You may hear more about ice-fishing for now-abundant herring in upcoming years as more places to catch them are discovered. Anglers occasionally catch cohos and chinooks in the same places.

Bobbing

If you scan Superior's frozen horizon in February, you'll see clusters of black specks far offshore.

Those are the impromptu teepee villages of bob-bers, some of the most adventurous ice-anglers you'll find anywhere. Bobbing (discussed on pages 78–80) is a very effective way to catch deepwater lake trout. The only prerequisite is stable ice con-ditions. Bobbers welcome Alberta clippers and prolonged cold snaps, because this is the weather Lake Superior needs to make ice. Bobbing is most popular in Wisconsin and the western U.P. The Bayfield area offers a good place for newcomers to start.

Late Winter Walleyes

In March and April, walleyes stage off the Supe-rior Entry—the natural mouth of the St. Louis River—as they ready for their spawning run. Cau-tious anglers brave the deteriorating ice conditions to catch them. The best fishing comes during low-light periods. The walleyes are usually on the bottom in water from twenty to fifty feet deep. Use your favorite walleye ice-fishing baits, prefer-ably tipped with a minnow, and don't be surprised if you catch an occasional lake trout or burbot.

Burbot

Marinas and Other Access Sites

FROM MAJOR PORTS like Duluth, Minnesota, to tiny hamlets such as Ontario's Rossport, Lake Superior offers a variety of places to launch your boat. While some towns are equipped with full-scale marinas, others provide only a launch ramp for small craft. Whatever size boat you plan to take out on the Big Pond, rest assured you can put in close to where you expect to find fish. A map indicating the major access sites of Lake Superior is on pages 104–105.

Minnesota

Minnesota's North Shore is exceptionally scenic, even by Lake Superior standards. High, forested ridges rise boldly from the shoreline. Aside from summer homes and several small communities, the coast remains undeveloped. In the winter, timber wolves walk the shoreline and the ice as they hunt for white-tailed deer.

This portion of the lake differs from the more hospitable South Shore in several ways. Shallow shoreline areas are rare because the bottom slopes quickly into water several hundred feet deep. Access is limited to a handful of sites, some of which are best suited to trailerable craft. Boaters find

> Whatever size boat you plan to take out on the Big Pond, rest assured you can put in close to where you expect to find fish.

little protection from wind and weather because few islands or sheltered coves exist along this rugged coast.

Summertime fishing along the North Shore follows a predictable pattern. The action begins in Duluth, where the water warms first, and then gradually moves north and eastward as the season progresses. By early August the best fishing is one hundred miles up the coast near Grand Marais. Then, in late August, lake trout and chinook salmon become more active as the spawning season approaches. September is usually a good month for trollers.

Duluth offers the amenities of a midsized city and good fishing. You can launch from the public access below the John Blatnik Bridge in the Duluth harbor and venture out through the Duluth ship canal, passing beneath the famous Aerial Bridge as you do so. Marina facilities and charter services are available. The best fishing action is in May, June, and September, although lake trout are caught all summer. If Lake Superior is too rough for fishing, you can explore the harbor and the St. Louis River, noted for excellent walleye fishing. The St. Louis also supports northern pike, crappies, smallmouth bass, and even some muskies.

About seventeen miles north of Duluth is the port of Knife River, where you'll find a full-service marina. Fishing around Knife River picks up somewhat later than off Duluth and lasts into July. Charters are available. The next port is Two Harbors, which has a large public access tucked behind the shelter of a harbor breakwall. Two Harbors is also a commercial port, and you'll see Great Lakes ore carriers loading at the huge docks. You can find excellent fishing during June, July, and September. Locals troll throughout the winter for cohos just out from the harbor. Because of the

> If Lake Superior is too rough for fishing, you can explore the Duluth harbor and the St. Louis River, noted for excellent walleye fishing.

difficulties in launching, small boats are the rule for winter trollers.

Shore-casters will find excellent shoreline access between Duluth and Two Harbors. Favorite fishing spots are the Canal Park piers in Duluth and the mouths of the Lester, French, and Knife Rivers. Expect good fishing in spring, early summer, and fall for a grab bag of species. Winter fishing for Kamloops rainbows is very popular, especially near the Lester and the French. Ice tent villages spring up off Duluth when ice conditions allow anglers to venture out in search of cohos, lake trout, and herring. In years with good ice, bobbers head far offshore to look for lake trout.

North of Two Harbors, you must travel to the city of Silver Bay to find another launch. A public ramp exists there now, and a full-scale marina is planned. Try trolling in June and July, but be prepared to run several miles to reach the fishing grounds. A taconite processing plant at Silver Bay discharges warm water that attracts a variety of trout and salmon. The scenery in this area is stunning. Be sure to troll west from the launch for an on-the-water view of famous Split Rock Lighthouse. Most of the shore-fishing in this area takes place near the mouths of rivers like the Stewart, Split Rock, Beaver, and Baptism.

Public ramps can be found at the communities of Schroeder and Tofte, which are about three miles apart, eighty miles up the coast from Duluth. Neither of these launches is sheltered, which limits their use to nice days. Plans are in the offing to build a better access somewhere in the vicinity. The best fishing here comes during July and August because the water is simply too cold earlier in the season. When the fish are in, trolling for cohos can be excellent. If the big lake is too rough for fishing, head inland on the Sawbill or Caribou

A taconite processing plant at Silver Bay discharges warm water that attracts a variety of trout and salmon. The scenery in this area is stunning.

trails—gravel forest roads—and sample the action in a myriad of inland lakes.

Grand Marais is the crown jewel of Minnesota's North Shore, a picturesque community poised on a small harbor. A tourist mecca, Grand Marais offers a wide range of things to see and do. You'll find two public launches and a small marina in the town's harbor. Charter services are available. In May and June, you can catch lake trout by fishing deep with downriggers. You'll find the best fishing in July and August, when the lake finally warms enough to make surface trolling possible. Often trollers find active fish just beyond the harbor breakwall, making Grand Marais an excellent choice for small boaters. The community also serves as the gateway to the famous Gunflint Trail, which leads sixty miles into the northern forests to mighty Saganaga Lake. You can fish inland lakes for walleyes, lake trout, or other species when Superior is unruly.

Just east of the tiny community of Hovland is the Horseshoe Bay public access site. Although more sheltered than the Schroeder and Tofte launch sites, Horseshoe Bay can challenge trollers with large, trailerable craft. Fishing is best here during July and August. The northernmost Minnesota port is Grand Portage, where you'll find two marinas on Grand Portage Bay. East of Grand Portage, the Susie Islands provide a great place to troll for lake trout and salmon in August. Further east is Pigeon Bay, which Minnesota shares with Ontario. Be sure to visit the famous Hole In The Wall, a tiny cove once used by smugglers. Although lake trout predominate, you might catch anything in Pigeon Bay—including occasional walleyes and whitefish. In late winter, brave ice-anglers venture out on the pack ice to fish for lake trout and whitefish.

Grand Marais is the crown jewel of Minnesota's North Shore, a picturesque community poised on a small harbor.

Grand Portage is a popular port with boaters bound for Isle Royale, which lies about twenty miles offshore. You can find charters to fish both locally and out at Isle Royale. Commercial ferry service, including transport for small boats and outboard motors, is also available.

Wisconsin

Wisconsin has the least shoreline on Lake Superior of any state or province, but some of the best fishing opportunities. If any place on Lake Superior can be described as basking in the sun, it is the South Shore. The southerly location, combined with extensive shoreline shallows, allows the waters to start warming here a month or more before they do on the North Shore. Many trollers kick off their season fishing from Wisconsin ports. However be sure to carefully read the fishing regulations, because most species have size and bag limits intended to sustain a quality fishing resource.

At the South Shore's western edge lies the city of Superior, a friendly community with a full-service marina at Barkers Island. A number of charter boats operate out of Superior. The Superior Entry to the Duluth-Superior harbor is the natural mouth of the St. Louis River. In the spring, shoreline erosion and flows from the clay-red Nemadji River, which runs into the bay, tint waters along the shore a muddy red. Trollers fish along the edge of the mud line for a potpourri of species, including chinooks, cohos, and lakers. Although the harbor offers good summer fishing for walleye and northern pike, boaters often travel east to the mouth of the Amnicon River or even the Bois Brule before setting out their lines. During the summer, trolling on the open lake for walleyes is becoming more popular.

The southerly location of Wisconsin's South Shore, combined with extensive shoreline shallows, allows the waters to start warming here a month or more before they do on the North Shore.

Deepwater trolling for lake trout is usually good, too.

Port Wing has a small marina and sheltered launch with charters available. This area is popular with small boaters because they can easily reach the fishing grounds and can catch fish near the surface throughout much of the fishing season. Spring surface-fishing for cohos and chinooks can be excellent; steelhead and browns are taken then, too. Lake trout are the bread and butter of the summer fishery, although brown trout show up in July and August as they prepare to enter tributary rivers to spawn. Summer fishing for walleyes averaging four to five pounds has been consistent in recent years. Look for walleyes near the mouths of the Brule and Iron Rivers. In the fall, watch for chinooks and cohos to begin moving near shore. A dodger and fly combination is a local favorite for autumn coho.

West of Port Wing the lake has a flat bottom and is relatively shallow. As you move east you can find deep water and associated shelves and bars within a half mile of shore. The water stays cold here well into July, and trollers off Herbster and Cornucopia are still catching fish in the top forty feet when anglers on the western end are resorting to bouncing bottom. Good areas include the ledges between Herbster and Bark Point, and Eagle Island Shoal east of Cornucopia. Shore-casting is good at Herbster and Cornucopia during the spring and fall. Check out the local sloughs and bays for northern pike. In the winter, the harbor areas offer some ice-fishing opportunities for splake and other species. In winters with good ice, offshore bobbing is excellent.

Bayfield, popular with sailors and yachters, is also the gateway to good fishing in the Apostle Islands. Complete marina services are available.

Lake trout are the bread and butter of the summer fishery, although brown trout show up in July and August as they prepare to enter tributary rivers to spawn.

However, anyone fishing here must be aware of the two large refuge areas where no fishing is allowed. These refuges are intended to protect spawning lake trout populations, and most agree that fishing has improved since they were established. You can find maps showing the location and coordinates of the refuge boundaries at local sport shops and the DNR office in Bayfield.

Fishing in the Apostles kicks off in May with topwater action for cohos and kings. Lake trout make up the bulk of the catch in June and throughout the summer. Brown trout weighing ten pounds or more are caught incidentally throughout the season, usually close to the island shorelines. You can find colder and clearer water farther out in the islands, and perhaps can locate active fish near the surface. During July and August, morning brings the best fishing. Bottom bouncing on the flats is a favorite technique. Lakers can run from fifteen to twenty-five pounds, and most of them are lean and taste good. Prime times for Apostle Islands lakers are from mid-June through mid-July and September. You can also catch them by bobbing during the winter.

It's an extremely windy day when you cannot fish on Chequamegon Bay. This lake within a lake is one of the best places for small boaters to sample Lake Superior fishing. Launches and marina services are available. Chequamegon's diverse fishery offers anglers a chance to catch just about any fish that swims in the lake. The west side of the bay is rocky; the east side has a muck bottom. Boaters take to the water at ice-out, often trolling among the ice floes to catch cohos, browns, and other species by flat-lining on the surface. Although the bay is one of the first places on the lake to start warming up in the spring, water temperatures can vary tremendously due to changing winds and

Brown trout weighing ten pounds or more are caught among the Apostle Islands incidentally throughout the season, usually close to the island shorelines.

currents. As summer progresses, trollers must move out into deeper water to find trout and salmon. However, fishing for species such as smallmouth bass and walleyes comes into its own, and you can find those smallmouth and walleyes in some atypical places. Fall brings trout and salmon back into the bay, and with the onset of winter comes good fishing for splake, browns, and lake trout. The hottest action is at first ice, usually around the first of the year.

Saxon Harbor, another popular trolling port, lies about two miles from the Michigan border. Some trollers get licenses from both states so they can fish off Michigan's Little Girl's Point. Offshore bobbing for lake trout is popular in the winter.

Michigan

Although Michigan has more miles of Lake Superior coastline than Minnesota and Wisconsin combined, fishing activity concentrates in certain places. One reason is that the Upper Peninsula is remote and has a small population, so traveling trollers are more likely to head for nearby Lake Michigan. Another is that commercial netting has depressed some local fish populations. Nevertheless, you can find good fishing.

The waters off Black River Harbor, in the west, consistently produce lake trout, although most are "fats." Spring fishing for cohos and browns is good near shore. At Ontanogan, anglers bounce bottom at 90 to 150 feet along a long sand flat for lake trout. In the spring they catch some steelhead, browns, and salmon. In the fall, you might find staging chinooks off the Ontanogan River.

Eagle Harbor and Copper Harbor on the Keweenaw Peninsula are good bets for lake trout throughout the season and salmon in the spring. Copper Harbor contains splake, which are fished

> Although Michigan has more miles of Lake Superior coastline than Minnesota and Wisconsin combined, fishing activity concentrates in certain places.

year-round. Anyone interested in a scenic winter adventure should sample the ice-fishing there.

In Traverse Harbor, you can catch lake trout and just about anything swimming in the lake by casting from the pier. Keweenaw Bay has a fishable lake trout population, but the majority of the fish are small enough to swim through the mesh of gill nets.

L'Anse is a favorite port for springtime trollers. Although abundant cohos used to be the draw, small chinooks have become more common in recent years. Some kings topping twenty pounds are boated, too. Look for the salmon near structure. In the summer, the salmon disappear. Nearby Huron Bay has a growing walleye population.

Marquette has a warmwater discharge that attracts cohos in the early spring. However, this port is primarily known for lake trout fishing. May is the best month to find lakers and a few salmon near the surface. In the summer, try fishing deep or bouncing the sandy bottom with spoons. Locals fish in the Marquette Harbor for northern pike and occasional trout and salmon. Some summer anglers like to fish for whitefish near the warmwater discharge.

Stannard Rock lies thirty-five miles offshore, a forty-two-mile run from Marquette. This is one of the few locations left on the Great Lakes where the native lake trout population is relatively intact. The area is best described as an underwater mountain range that breaks the surface in just two places, one of which is adorned with a lighthouse. Most anglers cast jigs on the reefs with medium spinning tackle. Some use twister tails (try white), while others tip their jigs with sucker minnows. Many anglers release the trophy fish they catch and keep only small fish for eating. Overfishing could damage this fragile lake trout population.

Michigan's Stannard Rock is one of the few locations left on the Great Lakes where the native lake trout population is relatively intact.

The Major Harbors and Access Sites of Lake Superior

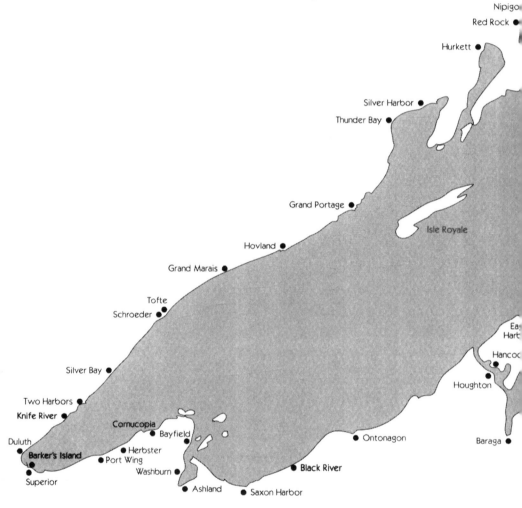

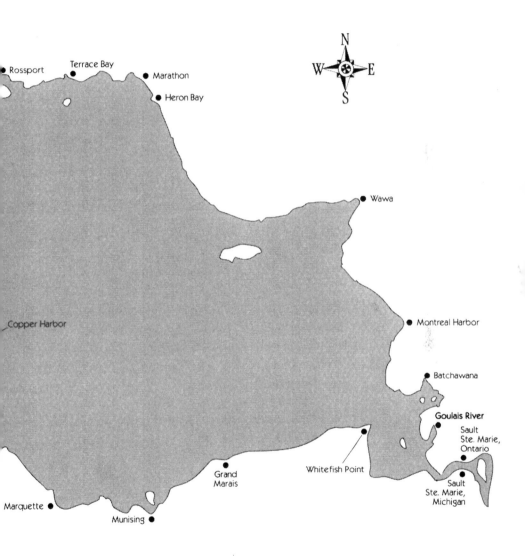

Good nearshore fishing is found from Marquette to Munising, including the waters around Grand and Wood Islands. Offshore northeast of Munising is Big Reef, noted for lake trout. Au Train offers a good place to troll for cohos and chinooks in the spring. You might also catch brown trout and splake in this area. In the winter, try fishing for cohos and whitefish through the ice in Munising Bay. To the east is the Pictured Rocks National Lakeshore. At Grand Marais's East Bay, anglers catch steelhead in the spring and fall near the mouth of the Sucker River. They fish for walleye and northern pike in Brimley Bay during the summer.

Isle Royale

Look on a map and it appears that Isle Royale should belong to Minnesota or Ontario, but it actually is part of Michigan. In fact, the Michigan border comes within a mile of Minnesota's Pigeon Point. The Island, as it is called by anglers, is a national park with no year-round human residents. Instead it is populated by moose and timber wolves.

Isle Royale's offshore waters provide a glimpse of what we've lost on Lake Superior. The reefs and shoals team with native lake trout, which survived the ravages of sea lampreys. Every summer, lake trout over thirty pounds are boated. One tipping the scales at a whopping forty-six pounds was caught in 1984. In the summer, you can catch cohos and chinooks offshore when you find the right water temperatures.

Getting to Isle Royale takes some doing. You must have a craft capable of making the open-water crossing. Isle Royale is about a twenty-mile run from Grand Portage, Minnesota, and about fifty miles from Eagle Harbor. Another option is to bring a small boat across on a ferry, although you must still exercise extreme caution when boating near the island. The National Park Service operates docks and campsites in several locations.

Although Isle Royale offers some of the best fishing you'll find *anywhere,* some fish managers, charter captains, and anglers are concerned that the slow-growing trophy lake trout cannot withstand heavy fishing pressure. Anglers should practice strict catch-and-release and keep only smaller fish for the table. "Filling the cooler" with monster lake trout is piggish. And even on waters as vast as Superior, there's no room for fish hogs.

The St. Marys River

The St. Marys River leaves Lake Superior at Sault Ste. Marie, and flows east to Lake Huron. This complex system's rapids, channels, locks, and lakes support a tremendous diversity of fish species. Where it leaves Lake Superior the water is cold and clear. Between the twin towns of Sault Ste. Marie, Michigan and Ontario, is a stretch known for excellent steelhead and salmon fishing. Most of the fish come from Lake Huron and are substantially larger than those typically caught in Lake Superior. An experimental Atlantic salmon

Consider a Charter

Many anglers would like to experience the fishing at Isle Royale, Stannard Rock, or other places on Lake Superior, but lack a suitable craft and equipment. They should consider hiring a charter captain for a half day, full day, or longer excursion. The captain not only has a boat but also has a wealth of fishing knowledge. A reliable captain will give you a comfortable and successful fishing trip—and that's worth paying for.

fishery has produced fish topping twenty pounds. Biologists suspect that pink and chinook salmon also may be hybridizing here, something never before documented in the wild. Angling for lake whitefish using small jigs or teardrops is fairly good in the spring. Farther downstream, the river flows around islands and through lakes. Lake George is noted for smallmouth bass and northern pike fishing. Lake Munuscong is better for walleyes and muskies.

Ontario

Ontario has the longest and the wildest Lake Superior shoreline. In places like Pukaskwa National Park and the Slate Islands, trollers occasionally see woodland caribou, members of Canada's southernmost caribou population, wandering along the shoreline. Access to the lake varies from excellent marinas in some communities to the roadless wilderness on the Pukaskwa Peninsula.

Starting on the east at Sault Ste. Marie is the St. Marys River, where the best access to the steelhead and salmon fishing areas is along the Ontario shore. Fishable numbers of trout and salmon occupy the river from September through June. About fifteen miles west of the Sault is Goulais Bay, where the spring smelt run draws schools of chinook salmon. Green and black are hot salmon colors. Another salmon hotspot extends from Lapointe's Point to Harmony Island off Batchawana Bay. The bay itself has good summer fishing for northern pike and smallmouth bass. Marina and launch facilities are available. Early summer surface fishing is good for lake trout and steelhead. Later on, you can fish deeper with downriggers.

You can launch at Montreal Harbor to fish Agawa Bay, a popular place for steelhead spring

One of Ontario's salmon hotspots extends from Lapointe's Point to Harmony Island off Batchawana Bay. The bay itself has good summer fishing for northern pike and smallmouth bass.

and fall. Michipicoten Harbor at Wawa has a marina. This area became a hot spot for chinooks during the 1980s, but catches have dropped off in recent years. However, lake trout fishing is excellent. From the mouth of the Michipicoten River you can head east along the remote Pukaskwa Peninsula. The gateway to Pukaskwa National Park is at Heron Bay, east of Marathon. Here you can launch at the mouth of the Pic River. If Superior is too rough for trolling, explore the lower river for walleyes. To the east is the mouth of the White River, another popular fishing area.

Marathon, a town of paper mills and gold mines, has a spectacular view of Lake Superior. Sight-seeing trollers should visit Coldwell Harbor, just a few miles to the west. Excellent fishing for lake trout and steelhead can be found among the numerous reefs, points, and islands. A natural fish-attracting location is the mouth of the mighty Steel River, located between Marathon and Terrace Bay. The only drawback is that getting there requires a long run along a frequently windy exposed shoreline.

The pleasant community of Terrace Bay has a launch ramp for small craft. The Slate Islands lie about six miles offshore. The Slates, like Isle Royale, offer lake trout fishing the way it used to be, as well as astounding scenery. Local charter captains offer day trips to the Slates. A few miles east, the tiny town of Rossport is sheltered among a maze of islands. The town has a good launch and dock, and may eventually build a marina. Although locals hit the water in May when the ice goes out, the fishing doesn't really pick up until mid-June, when flat-lining for lake trout is very productive. In July, steelhead are common catches, with cohos, chinooks, and the odd Atlantic salmon tossed in for spice.

Ontario's Slate Islands, like Michigan's Isle Royale, offer lake trout fishing the way it used to be, as well as astounding scenery.

Rossport has a long fishing history; originally it was famous for commercial lake trout fishing. The offshore islands provide small boaters with shelter, and fish are usually found in the top thirty or forty feet of water throughout the summer season. Smelt are the primary bait fish, although chubs and herring predominate in the open water off the islands. Because the islands are actually the peaks of underwater mountains, you'll find reefs and other structure everywhere. However, be sure to work the bug lines and temperature breaks, too. Flutter spoons are favorites. Good colors are silver and lime for lakers, orange or red for steelhead, and black and strawberry for salmon.

West of Rossport, Nipigon Bay is sheltered from the main lake by the mass of St. Ignace Island. You'll find good trolling for lake trout, steelhead, and the occasional coaster brook trout until July, when the waters of the bay warm up. Then the best fishing is in the open lake beyond the islands. Sizable northern pike also swim in the bay.

The town of Nipigon, which has a new, full-service marina, sits on the banks of the lower Nipigon River. The Nipigon hosts resident and migrant populations of lake trout, brook trout, and rainbows, as well as a substantial fall salmon run. Trollers venture out for salmon and lake trout in Nipigon Bay and on the open lake, via the Nipigon Straits. Nearby Red Rock also has a new marina. The shorelines along the Black Bay Peninsula produce coaster brook trout in the spring. Try flat-lining with small spoons or casting spinners tipped with worms into shoreline structures.

Thunder Bay has public launches and full marina services. Trollers here talk about the chinook salmon fishery that has developed following large stockings in the Kaministiquia River. The

In Thunder Bay, trollers credit large stockings in the Kaministiquia River for the developing chinook salmon fishery.

bay also has a terrific lake trout population; the only drawback is that they aren't very good to eat. The Sleeping Giant, a thousand-foot rocky ridge at the tip of the Sibley Peninsula, protects the bay from lake storms. If you venture out of the bay to explore the numerous fjordlike coves along the coast, travel in a seaworthy craft with ample fuel supplies. The coast from Thunder Bay to the Minnesota border is reminiscent of Isle Royale, which lies just offshore.

Stream Fishing

ANGLERS—AND EVERYONE ELSE—in the Lake Superior country welcome spring. After a long winter, warm days and the sound of running water are welcome indeed. Perhaps that's why spring steelhead fishing in Lake Superior tributary streams is so popular. Steelhead make their spawning run into the streams shortly after ice-out, which makes them one of the first fish species available to open-water anglers. Because nearly every creek and river flowing into Lake Superior has the cold water and habitat necessary to support trout, steelhead are easily accessible to anglers all around the lake.

This doesn't mean steelhead are easy to catch. Steelheading requires angling skill and the ability to "read the water." However, accomplished steelheaders can use their techniques to catch all of the migratory trout and salmon species that enter the rivers at various times of year. Most steelheaders contend that stream fishing is the most exciting way to fish for Lake Superior trout and salmon. In addition, many watersheds offer excellent fishing for smaller resident brook, brown, and rainbow trout. To those who hear music in the click and whir of a fly reel, Lake Superior's tributaries offer endless fishing opportunities.

Most steelheaders contend that stream-fishing is the most exciting way to fish for Lake Superior trout and salmon.

The Rivers

For the angler, Lake Superior streams can be placed in two broad categories: fast-moving and slow-moving. A rugged ridge of hills borders most of the lake's North Shore from Duluth to Sault Ste. Marie. The North Shore rivers tumble quickly down rocky valleys, in a series of rapids and pools. On the South Shore, streams generally have less gradient and are slower moving, although anyone familiar with these rivers can point out many places where you'll find rapids and waterfalls.

Streams on the northern and southern coasts have different characteristics. North Shore streams originate in swamps or inland lakes. Most support populations of wild brook trout in the upper reaches, although some—particularly those beginning in or flowing through lakes—have cool-water species such as walleyes, northern pike, and small-mouth bass. The flow in most North Shore streams depends on runoff. The rivers run high from snow melt or rain, and nearly dry up during low-flow periods in late summer and winter. This variation in flow also leads to wide fluctuations in water temperature. The streams become super-chilled (32 or 33 degrees) during winter and may warm to 70 degrees or more during the summer dog days. For trout, and anglers, the best water temperatures and stream flows are during the runoff period of spring and early summer, and following autumn rains.

The granite ridgetops where North Shore streams originate are over one thousand feet higher than Lake Superior's elevation of 602 feet above sea level. Minnesota's Eagle Mountain, for instance, lies about ten miles inland from the lake and has an elevation of 2,301 feet. This means that many streams have numerous cascades and waterfalls. On the North Shore, most streams have a waterfall within a mile of the lake that is high enough to block the upstream migration of fish. Fishing for migratory trout and salmon is restricted to the portion of river below the waterfall. However, don't underestimate the athletic prowess of fish, especially wild steelhead. They have adapted to these rugged streams and can leap four feet or higher. It takes a mighty cataract to stop these fish.

On the South Shore, spawning trout and salmon can swim all the way to the headwaters of many streams, especially those flowing through clays and sandy soils. Many South Shore streams are spring-fed and thus have more constant flows and consistent water temperatures. They are biologically more productive, with a greater abundance and diversity of insects and other aquatic life, as well as substantial gravel-bottomed areas providing fish spawning and nursery areas.

These South Shore streams, as well as some of Ontario's large rivers, are important spawning areas for wild populations of steelhead, coho, and chinook salmon, brown trout, and brook trout. These wild fish make up a substantial proportion of Lake Superior's fishery, so the protection of these fragile trout streams is vital.

Getting The Drift

Large trout and salmon usually enter tributary streams to spawn. Because they are focused on mating rather than feeding, these fish seem difficult to catch. Fish are not likely to sip dry flies from the surface or to pursue fast-moving lures in the cold waters of spring and fall. However, they will strike a properly presented bait—one that is drifting with the current near the bottom. This simple fact is the foundation for drift-fishing.

Drifting with bait or artificial flies—the most

common fishing technique used for steelhead and other species—is not only effective but also allows anglers to use inexpensive terminal gear. Every trout stream's bottom has a mixture of bait-grabbing logs, rocks, and natural debris. Frequent snags are a fact of life, and the average angler could lose a small fortune of expensive artificial lures during a day's fishing. By contrast, a hook, sinker, and spawn bag cost just pennies, which makes snagging up and breaking off your line much less painful.

A good drift-angler also has excellent line control. That angler can drift a bait *exactly* where the fish hold and can detect even the lightest strikes. To the novice, an expert drifter may seem to have almost mystical abilities. Steelheaders say an expert has "the touch," a combination of quick reflexes and stream experience.

Duluth-area drift anglers have honed their tackle and techniques to perfection during the last

Brook Trout Heaven

Travel far enough upstream on virtually every Lake Superior tributary and you'll discover brook trout water. Cold creeks and beaver ponds are the places that brookies (or specks, as the Canadians say) call home. In some streams, where historically brook trout were able to swim upstream from the lake unimpeded by natural barriers, the trout have always been there. On others, where cascades and cataracts blocked migration routes, brook trout were stocked in the headwaters. Either way, most of the brook trout you catch will be wild fish. Headwater brook trout populations suffer from benign neglect by both fish managers and anglers. Very little stocking is being done, and brook trout populations in some streams were wiped out or seriously damaged in recent drought years.

In some instances, these piscatorial tragedies have gone unnoticed simply because few anglers pursue brook trout anymore. And that's just fine with those who do. Brook trout anglers are solitary types, who prefer the

sixty years. Because most Lake Superior tributaries are small to medium-sized streams, the ability to cast long distances is unnecessary. Instead of spinning or casting tackle, drifters use a fly rod and monofilament line. Since sinkers are invariably used to bring the bait near the bottom, the line is flipped out instead of cast. With a little practice, you can become very accurate to distances of forty feet or more.

The key to effective drift-fishing is using enough weight to pull the bait to the bottom and yet still allow it to drift with the current. The angler then keeps a tight line to feel when the sinker occasionally touches bottom as it drifts along and to detect strikes. Often the strike is no more than a light tap or a stop in the drift. Trout and salmon often quickly reject the bait, so it is important to set the hook immediately.

The graphite fly rods most drifters use are eight

company of moose over humans when they are fishing. Lots of wild country remains throughout the Lake Superior Basin, and brook trout creeks flow through most of it.

Brook trout are not as gullible as some anglers claim, but they are easy to catch. Most locals just drift a tiny hook baited with an earthworm or minnow and weighted with tiny split shot through the pools. Some cast tiny spinners or crappie jigs with ultralight spinning gear. Others prefer to fish with flies, matching wits with wild trout on tranquil beaver ponds or larger streams. Regardless of the method, the result is the same—vividly colored brookies hardly larger than the spoons some trollers use on the Big Pond. But brook trout anglers measure their quarry on a different scale. Keep your chrome-bright monsters, they say, and give us fresh brook trout for breakfast.

to nine feet in length and rated for 7-to 9-weight
fly lines, rods light enough to allow finesse yet
strong enough to handle ten-pound fish. Most
drifters prefer single action fly reels with adjust-
able drags. It is not uncommon to see a steelheader
climb out of a five-hundred dollar pickup truck
with a three-hundred dollar fly rod. Quality tackle
not only is more effective but is a delight to use.

Most anglers prefer high-quality abrasion-resistant monofilament line from 6- to 12-pound
test, with 8-pound the norm. In low and clear
water the fish may be line shy, but more often the
line must be strong enough to stand up to the
rigors of battling powerful fish in strong currents.
Steelhead are never simply cranked in.

Drifters require only a few essential tools.
Aside from a fly rod and reel, a drifter needs only
chest or hip waders, a fishing vest for carrying
tackle, and a large-hooped landing net with
weighted mesh. Many anglers prefer neoprene
waders for standing in cold water. Nonslip felt
soles provide surefooted traction for wading on
the slippery rocks that pave many stream bottoms. A fishing vest should be well constructed,
with large sturdy pockets, because a box of sinkers weighs more than a box of dry flies. Landing
nets must be large enough to accomodate a ten-
pound trout, and a weighted mesh is easier to
use in a current.

Spawn, Yarn, Etc.

Most drifters use spawn or a spawn imitation when
fishing for trout and salmon. Anglers have all sorts
of theories about why basically nonfeeding spawners will strike a bait or lure. Some say fish strike
from aggression; others say, from a feeding instinct.
The bottom line is that all species of trout and
salmon will bite during a spawning run and that,

although other baits can be tried, spawn or an imitation works best most of the time.

Most anglers collect trout or salmon spawn from the fish they catch. Ripe spawn—eggs ready to be laid—is preferred because it is the easiest to prepare. After removing the spawn from the fish, pull away the skein membranes and wash the spawn in cold water to remove blood and offal. Place the spawn in a collander or on paper towels to drain. Then lightly sprinkle it with borax to preserve it. (Don't use too much borax, or the spawn will dry out.) Spawn treated in such a manner keeps well in the refrigerator or can be frozen for later use.

Most anglers tie the spawn in small mesh sacks about the size of a thumbnail. You can buy suitable mesh at sporting goods shops. Cut the mesh into three-inch squares. Place some eggs in the center of the square (a little practice will indicate the proper amount), then gather the corners of the mesh to form a small, round sack. Use a strong thread (Kevlar fly-tying thread works well) to tie off the sack, securing it with two or three tight half hitches. Even a ten-thumbed tyro should be able to tie enough spawn sacks for a weekend's fishing in an hour or so. Don't make the sacks too big—no larger than the diameter of a quarter. Even huge trout more readily strike small baits than large ones. In drift fishing, the old adage about big baits for big fish doesn't apply.

Some anglers preserve "tight" (unripe) spawn in the skein with borax and then cut it into small chunks. This "loose" spawn is then secured to the hook using a snell knot with an egg loop. Loose spawn may be somewhat more effective for finicky fish, but it is difficult to keep on the hook. When the water is cold or when streams are low and clear, some anglers prefer to use light line, a

Anglers have all sorts of theories about why non-feeding spawners will strike a bait or lure. Some say fish strike from aggression; others say, from a feeding instinct.

tiny hook, and a single salmon egg. Preserved salmon eggs can be purchased at sporting goods stores.

Spawn sacks are durable, and have the double attractions of appearance and scent. Run a NO. 6 or NO. 4 hook just below the knot in the sack, taking care not to puncture the eggs. Some anglers use spawn in conjunction with a fluorescent yarn fly or douse the sack with fish-attracting scent. Drift the bait along the bottom in likely holding areas. The strike is usually a solid tap. Set the hook immediately, before the fish rejects the bait. The bait is rarely taken deep, so trout and salmon caught on spawn can be easily released.

Although anglers who fish slow to moderate currents prefer spawn sacks, this bait is difficult to use in snag-infested fast streams. That's why most fast-water anglers prefer to use yarn flies. The yarn fly is so small and simple that many novices refuse to believe it catches fish. It is just a pea-sized puff of fluorescent yarn attached to a small hook with a snell knot. Like traditional artificial flies, it resembles a natural food, a free-drifting

Alternative Baits

Many anglers swear by spawn, but other baits catch fish, too. Nightcrawlers will entice brown trout and brookies, as well as steelhead. Often, though, just a piece of 'crawler is more effective than the entire worm, because trout prefer small and medium-sized baits when in a stream.

When available, mayfly wigglers and stonefly nymphs are deadly, especially in cold, slow-moving water. Wigglers can be purchased in some bait shops along the South Shore in winter and spring. You can catch your own stonefly nymphs by turning over rocks in shallow riffles. Don't be greedy when collecting bait because these nymphs are important trout foods.

trout or salmon egg. But the yarn fly has advantages over natural eggs: it stays on the hook and it can be tied in various colors to suit the water conditions—or the angler's mood.

Fishing with yarn was refined to an art on the fast streams near Duluth. Over the years, Duluth-area drifters have tried fishing with yarn most everywhere that steelhead and salmon swim, including the Pacific Northwest. The technique is generally more effective than local methods, especially in moderate to fast currents. Now it is possible to buy Glow Bugs—pretied yarn flies—in fly-fishing catalogs.

Yarn performs best in fast, rocky streams where migrating fish lie in small pockets behind rocks or in depressions on the bottom. Using the right amount of split shot, you can get a yarn fly to the bottom quickly and, with practice, drift it exactly where the fish should be holding. So precise is this method that a skilled drifter can often feel fish brush against the line.

Unfortunately, a novice may feel nothing other than the tick-tick of the sinkers bouncing along the bottom. Trout and salmon rarely wallop yarn, but instead inhale it. The indication of a strike may be no more than a slight pause in the drift. You must have a tight line in order to control the drift and feel strikes. Setting the hook is done, as in fly-fishing, by quickly cocking your wrist.

With practice, you can quickly tie yarn flies on the stream. The key is knowing how to tie a snell knot (see page 122), which requires an up-eyed hook. The most popular hooks are salmon egg or steelhead hooks in sizes 4 or 6, which can be purchased in quantity. In a snell knot, the line passes through the eye of the hook and is wrapped around the shank. This allows direct pull when you set the hook.

Tying A
Snelled Yarn Fly

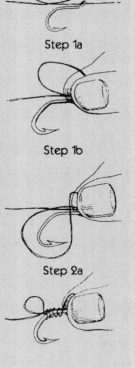

1. Thread the line through the eye of the hook and form a loop above the shank (1a). Pinch the shank and the eye of the hook with your thumb and forefinger (1b).

2. Using the top portion of the loop, wind the line around the shank of the hook and itself (2a). Make five to seven turns. Be sure to keep pinching the loop with your thumb and forefinger (2b).

3. Tighten the knot on the hook shank by pulling the main line and the tag end. Wet the line with your tongue so the knot seats properly.

4. Now there is a small gap between the knot and the eye of the hook. Insert a one-inch piece of yarn between the line and the hook shank. Then use your thumb and forefinger to slide the knot to the hook eye.

5. Pinch the yarn between your thumb and forefinger, and use a small scissors to trim it to the size of a pea. Be careful not to cut your line!

Step 1a

Step 1b

Step 2a

Step 2b

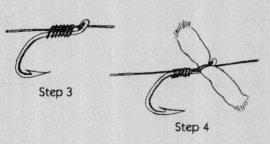

Step 3

Step 4

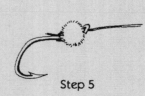

Step 5

Yarn for making yarn flies is widely available at sporting good shops throughout the Lake Superior region. It comes in an array of colors, although fluorescent shades of orange and green are most commonly used. Generally speaking, fluorescent green is most effective when the water is cold, high, or discolored. Fluorescent orange works best in average fishing conditions. Lighter shades of orange and pink will fool fish when the water is low and clear, conditions often found toward the end of the spring steelhead run.

Those who cannot tie their own yarn flies can purchase pretied ones from tackle retailers, although these must often be trimmed to the proper small size. Another suitable imitation is rubber salmon eggs or egg clusters; sometimes, these are impregnated with fish-attracting scent. As always, the addition of scent increases your chances of catching fish.

A Weighty Issue

When the water is clear, you can often see steelhead lying in holding areas. Drifting to visible fish can teach you a lot about this fishing method. If, for instance, you make several drifts and the fish ignores your offering, add more weight. Often this is all it takes to put the bait in front of the fish and draw a strike. Learning to use the proper amount of weight is the most important part of drift fishing.

Most drifters use split shot sinkers they purchase in bulk quantities. However, with the current national efforts to ban lead fishing sinkers, drifters may soon be searching for a substitute—and rightly so. Serious drifters go through pounds of lead each season.

Sinkers are attached to the line in a couple of different ways. Some anglers use a dropper system. They attach a small barrel swivel to the main line, and then run a lighter leader to the hook. The leader may be anywhere from twelve to over thirty-six inches long, although sixteen to eighteen inches will suffice in most situations. Another short line is tied to the swivel (some use the tag end of the leader) as a dropper for the sinkers. Split shot or other pinch-on weights are attached to the dropper. If the sinkers hang up, they slide off the dropper line when you pull free so that you save the rest of the rig.

Other anglers pinch the split shot directly on their lines. Although you may lose more hooks, you can quickly retie. With this method you have only one knot at the hook; the dropper system has an additional two knots at the barrel swivel. Knots are the weak link in any fishing setup, an important consideration when fishing for super-charged lake-run fish.

Deciding on the proper amount of weight for a given situation takes practice. The goal is to get your bait drifting along the bottom at the same speed as the current. If you hang up frequently, you're probably using too much lead. If you can't feel the sinkers bouncing on the bottom, add more weight. An experienced drifter can work through snaggy areas with minimal hang-ups, but a novice should plan on getting lots of practice in tying snell knots.

Slip Shot Sinkers on a Dropper Line

Timing Is Everything

Duck hunters know the importance of timing. If you're on the marsh when the flights come in, you'll shoot ducks. Otherwise, you may stare at empty skies. This holds true for drift fishing, too. Trout and salmon make their spawning runs when the time of year and water conditions are right. That's when you should be fishing.

Steelhead make their spring run when water

temperatures reach forty degrees. A few fish may begin entering the streams in late winter, but they will be sluggish and difficult to catch. Generally, the steelhead run peaks in mid-April along the South Shore and as late as mid-May on the North Shore. Strong runs are often triggered by the first warm spring rains.

Steelhead also make a fall run in some of the larger tributaries. In streams such as Wisconsin's Bois Brule, these fish spend the winter in the river and then spawn in the early spring. Although you can catch steelhead in the rivers during September, you'll find the best numbers from October to freeze-up. Fall-run steelhead are generally more aggressive and harder fighters than spring-run fish.

Chinook salmon may start entering the rivers as early as July, but the best fishing is generally from Labor Day until mid-October. Because most streams are at low levels in the fall, the best salmon runs usually coincide with rains. However, on most Lake Superior streams you can usuallycount on finding fishable numbers of chinooks during the last two weeks of September. After the first of October, many chinooks you catch will have begun to deteriorate.

Brown trout and brook trout, both fall spawners, enter certain tributary streams during August and September. Both species are relatively uncommon in Lake Superior. The best-known brown trout run is in Wisconsin's Bois Brule River, although most South Shore streams receive at least a few browns. On the North Shore browns are uncommon. Brook trout run a handful of rivers on the Ontario coast, of which the largest and best known is the Nipigon River. These native fish are few in number, and anyone who fishes for them should practice strict catch-and-release.

Coho salmon are late autumn spawners. Some

Chinook salmon may start entering the rivers as early as July, but the best fishing is generally from Labor Day until mid-October.

of the best runs occur just before freeze-up, when most anglers are deer hunting instead. Like chinooks, cohos die after spawning, although they deteriorate less quickly. Several South Shore rivers, particularly Wisconsin's better trout streams, receive fishable runs. However, a late fall drifter might stumble into a run of cohos on just about any stream. Cohos will travel all the way to headwater creeks to spawn.

Although they do not spawn in streams, lake trout occasionally run the rivers in the fall. Look for them following autumn rains when the water temperatures drop below fifty degrees. Atlantic salmon appear in the rivers in September and October, although you may also catch them in late May near the end of the steelhead run. Pink salmon show up during the latter half of September, with the initial run typically following a rain. If you can catch these small salmon as they're entering the river, they'll bite readily and have edible flesh. However, they quickly deteriorate, becoming difficult to catch and inedible.

Like A Novel

A river is like a good novel. Just as a good reader gets more out of the story, a good stream angler catches more fish by "reading the water." This essential skill is one you can hone only with experience, although the basics are easy enough to understand. When in a stream, trout and salmon invariably face upstream so they can watch for food drifting downstream and be alert to danger. Unless actively feeding or spawning, they are rarely far from cover.

The skillful angler is stealthy and, noting the day's conditions, focuses on places where the fish are most likely to be. If it is cold, the trout lie in the deep holes. On sunny days, they seek shade.

> Atlantic salmon appear in the rivers in September and October, although you may also catch them in late May near the end of the steelhead run.

If a spawning run is in progress, they may "stack up" at waterfalls or other obstacles to migration. Species behave differently from each other. Chinooks, for instance, seem to congregate in the deepest water available. Steelhead like to hold in the heads and tails of pools. Brown trout seek refuge beneath overhanging brush.

Reading a rough-and-tumble river isn't easy, particularly because the best fishing often comes when water levels are high. Some streams, especially on the North Shore, appear to be no more than chasms filled with unrelenting white water. However, look more closely and you'll see many places where fish can find shelter from the strong current. These may be pockets in the rapids, pools, or slower currents along the edges of fast runs.

The bottoms of many Lake Superior tributaries consist of nothing other than big rocks and little rocks, because spring freshets and summer torrents flush out everything that isn't heavy enough to withstand the current. On some streams, you can actually hear boulders rolling along the bottom when the water is high. Rocks, then, become important to trout and salmon, and to the anglers who pursue them.

Let's take a look at a typical river rock. We'll put it at midstream, breaking a fast current. A long eddy with a cobblestone and gravel bottom forms downstream from our rock, giving migrating trout slower currents where they can hold, rest, and perhaps even spawn. A small pocket of slower water also forms ahead of the rock where the current pushes against it.

Trout might hold in the pocket in front of the rock, nose up to it from behind, or lie in the eddy ten feet or more behind it. The only way you'll know is by making a few drifts. Unless the water is low and the fish are spooky, it's usually best to

On some streams, you can actually hear boulders rolling along the bottom when the water is high.

approach a rock from upstream and fish down past it. Start by drifting your bait above the rock, then work the current edges along the sides of the rock and the pocket behind it. Then fish the slow waters that extend downstream, paying particular attention to the current edges and the tailout where the current begins to pick up speed.

Always remember the places where you hook fish, because you may find others there in the future. Prime holding areas consistently attract fish. You can extend this theory further when you explore new waters. Look for places similar to spots where you've caught fish on familiar streams.

> Always remember the places where you hook fish, because you may find others there in the future. Prime holding areas consistently attract fish.

Pools are always worth a few drifts. A typical pool can be divided into three segments: head, midsection, and tail. All three portions hold trout at various times, although many anglers concentrate on the heads and tails. The heads of most pools have fast currents rushing over slower water. Trout move into these places to find shelter from the current and cover. Fish holding at the head are often ready biters.

The pool's tailout is a prime location to find undisturbed fish, perhaps even spawning pairs. Because the water is often shallow, you must approach the tail cautiously and make every drift count. Tailouts are also a good bet when the water is high and fish are running, because trout migrating upstream often hold in the tail when they enter a pool.

The midsections of pools also hold fish, although they may be difficult to catch. This is usually the deepest part of the hole, a place where fish hide when spooked by anglers. Try to fish near rocks or other cover. How can you locate rocks in a deep hole? Underwater disturbances appear as upwellings or boils in smooth currents. The rock creating the boil will be a few feet further upstream.

Another way to find rocks is by hanging up on them. If you keep snagging in the same place, most likely a large rock is the culprit. Change your drift until you can fish around it without hanging up.

If you want to get to know your favorite stream better, explore it during the summer, when the water is low. Look for rocks, deep pockets, and other "fishy" places. Then try those spots when the run is on. Also, if you pick a particular stretch of river and stick with it, you'll eventually learn where the fish hold when the water is high or low. Each fish you catch will make it easier to hook the next one.

Of course, you have to take this fishing seriously. If you want to become a successful drifter, you have to be on the stream as often as possible. That means setting aside weekends and vacation time. If you live nearby, go fishing before or after work. Plan on losing some sleep when the run is on. You may end up with bloodshot eyes, but that's a small price to pay for catching a trophy fish.

The Major Tributaries

HUNDREDS OF RIVERS AND STREAMS feed the greatest Great Lake, and they also provide a natural spawning ground for salmon and trout. Consequently, you will find some of the best fishing associated with Lake Superior on these tributaries.

Minnesota

The streams along Minnesota's North Shore are noted more for their scenic beauty than for their fishing potential. Nearly every tributary stream has within a mile of its mouth a large waterfall that blocks the upstream migrations of anadromous fish. In past years, the Minnesota DNR dynamited pockets into the rocky cascades of some streams so that strong leapers such as steelhead could negotiate them. This gave anadromous spawners access to additional stream mileage. Most Minnesota streams depend on runoff, which means that flows vary from flood stage in the spring and after rains to trickles during the summer.

Despite the difficulties that fish face, these rivers provide good fishing. Because the streams are fast and rocky, drifters have refined their techniques out of necessity. Having the proper gear and knowing how to use it are the keys to success.

Starting at Duluth, the first sizable tributary

Nearly every tributary stream along Minnesota's North Shore has within a mile of its mouth a large waterfall that blocks the upstream migrations of anadromous fish.

Major Tributaries Along Minnesota's North Shore

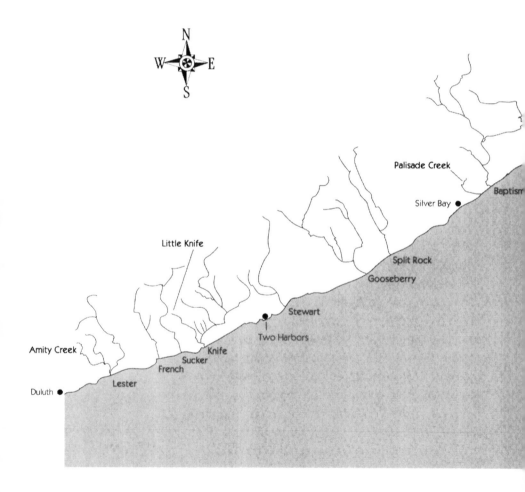

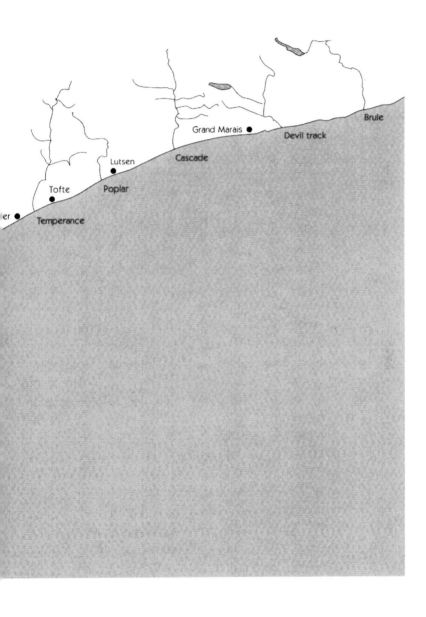

The Knife River is Minnesota's largest and best known steelhead stream, with about seventy miles of water available to spawning fish.

is the Lester River on the outskirts of town. The Lester receives strong runs of steelhead and Kamloops in the spring and chinook salmon in the fall. Because of its proximity to Duluth, it is usually crowded during peak fishing times. The Sucker River has more mileage available for fish and anglers and better absorbs heavy fishing pressure.

The Knife River is Minnesota's largest and best known steelhead stream, with about seventy miles of water available to spawning fish. However, in the past decade steelhead runs on the Knife have declined, and the fishery is merely a shadow of its former self. Anglers and fishery managers are working to restore the once-famous steelhead run. The Knife takes some salmon in autumn, but frequently low water levels make fishing difficult.

North of Two Harbors, the Stewart, Gooseberry, and Split Rock Rivers offer good stream access and spring steelhead. The Baptism River, in Tettegouche State Park near Silver Bay, is a large river stocked with chinook salmon. A number of deep holes hold kings and help spread out the salmon fishing crowds. Near Tofte, the Temperance River has a very short length accessible to lake-run fish. This river is no longer stocked with chinooks.

The Cascade River in Cascade State Park has consistent runs of steelhead in the spring and salmon in the fall. Less than a quarter mile of the river is accessible to the fish, with the upstream barrier being a deep hole beneath a dramatic waterfall. Here tourists can watch anglers battle with anadromous spawners. North of Grand Marais, the Devil Track and Brule (not to be confused with Wisconsin's Bois Brule) Rivers each offer over a mile of fishable water. Both flow through rugged canyons and are difficult and dangerous to fish, particularly when spring flows are running strong.

Of course, there are dozens of smaller, lesser known Minnesota tributaries. Virtually all are visited by steelhead in the spring; and when the right conditions exist, some receive fall salmon runs. Most of the land along these streams is public or is accessible to anglers. Private property is usually marked with signs. Respect the landowners and don't trespass.

Wisconsin

If heaven has a trout stream, it probably looks like Wisconsin's Bois Brule River. The Brule is arguably the finest trout stream in the Lake Superior drainage, providing not only good fishing for migrant steelhead, brown trout, and cohos but also excellent fly-fishing for resident brown and brook trout. Originating in a series of cold springs, the Brule flows north for nearly sixty miles through a valley shaded by cedar and towering white pines.

Unlike many Lake Superior tributaries, the spring-fed Brule maintains constant flows and water temperatures. This makes the river more attractive to steelhead, many of which enter the river in the fall, spend winter there, and then spawn in the early spring. Other steelhead run the river during April. The Brule also has a sizeable, healthy population of brown trout, fall spawners that start upstream in August and September. Both steelhead and browns topping ten pounds are not uncommon. Although the Brule has a modest annual chinook run, it is a major producer of coho salmon. The cohos run the river in the fall, traveling to distant headwater areas to spawn.

Most of the fishing for anadromous fish takes place in the lower twenty miles of river south of U.S. Highway 2. This area has extended spring and fall seasons. Above Highway 2, the river remains the domain of fly-fishers. The Brule has a

If heaven has a trout stream, it probably looks like Wisconsin's Bois Brule River, arguably the finest trout stream in the Lake Superior drainage.

Major Tributaries Along
Wisconsin's South Shore

Herbster

Duluth

Port Wing

Iron

Cranberr

Superior

Flag

Bois Brule

Nemadji

N
W   E
S

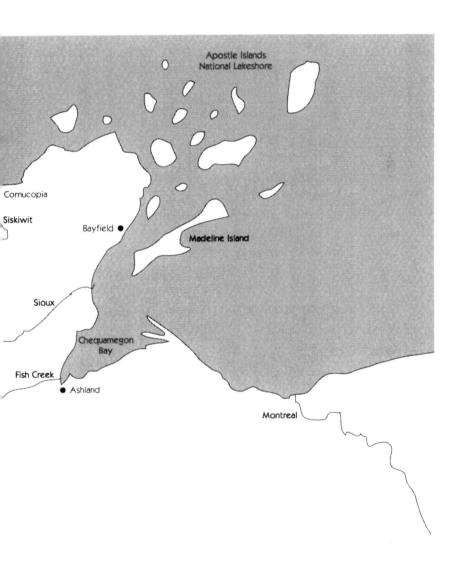

Apostle Islands
National Lakeshore

Cornucopia

Siskiwit

Bayfield ●

Madeline Island

Sioux

Chequamegon
Bay

Fish Creek

● Ashland

Montreal

long fly-fishing tradition that goes all the way back to the time when it was possible to catch a barrelful of brook trout on a day's outing. Today we no longer measure our catch by the barrel or bucket, and most conscientious anglers practice catch-and-release. Nevertheless, if one wades the Brule on a still June evening as the mayflies begin to hatch, it is not hard to imagine what the river was like in those early years. Expect to catch brook trout to twelve inches and browns to eighteen inches or more. Use a canoe (rentals are available) to explore the secluded upper river. Stone's Bridge provides a popular access

Wisconsin's other tributaries lack the classic appeal of the Brule, but nevertheless provide interesting fishing opportunities. The muddy Nemadji, which enters the St. Louis River estuary not far from the Superior Entry, is locally known for June walleye fishing. In spring and fall, steelhead and brown trout run up the Nemadji to spawn in clear, cold tributaries far upstream. Wisconsin and Minnesota share the upper Nemadji watershed.

The Iron and Flag Rivers near Port Wing take spring and fall runs. A dam on the lower Iron blocks upstream migrations, but fish have access to long stretches of the brushy Flag. Herbster's Cranberry River is somewhat larger and easier to fish, although its slow currents might stymie some drifters. The Sioux and Onion Rivers, which enter Chequamegon Bay south of Bayfield, are good bets for spring steelhead.

Ashland's Fish Creek looks more like a duck marsh than a trout stream, but you can catch steelhead there in the spring and browns and salmon in the fall.

Ashland's Fish Creek looks more like a duck marsh than a trout stream, but you can catch steelhead there in the spring and browns and salmon in the fall. The Montreal River, on the Michigan border, has only a short stretch of water available to Lake Superior migrants.

Michigan

Many streams drain the Upper Peninsula, but some are significantly better than others for fishing. On the western end, steelhead, chinooks, cohos, and browns congregate in large, deep holes on the Black River. Only a short stretch of river is available to lake migrants, but regular stockings assure consistent runs. Another river with very limited fishing area is the Presque Isle, west of the Porcupine Mountains. However, the scenery makes up for the fishing.

The Ontonagon River is a large, slow-flowing stream stocked with chinooks. About six or seven miles of river is accessible to small boaters. If you can't find any chinooks, you might be able to catch some walleyes. North of L'Anse, the Huron River has spring runs of wild and stocked steelhead. This river is considered one of the best steelhead streams in the western U.P.

Another stream worth investigating is the Chocolay River near Marquette. A large, relatively slow-moving river, the Chocolay hosts steelhead (and steelheaders) from autumn through spring. This is one of the few Lake Superior tributaries that is open to fishing and is fishable throughout the winter. Brown trout and Pacific salmon spice the autumn action. The Sucker River, entering the lake at Grand Marais, has several miles of steelhead water flowing through state land. The best fishing comes in the spring, although some chinooks ascend the river during the fall. Late autumn steelheading can be good.

Ernest Hemingway wrote about the Big Two-Hearted River, but that sly trout fisherman actually meant another stream. And he was fishing for brook trout, not steelhead. The *real* Two-Hearted is a fine steelhead stream that, much to the dismay of its longtime friends, is being discovered

North of L'Anse, the Huron River has spring runs of wild and stocked steelhead. This river is considered one of the best steelhead streams in the western U.P.

Major Tributaries Along
Michigan's Shoreline

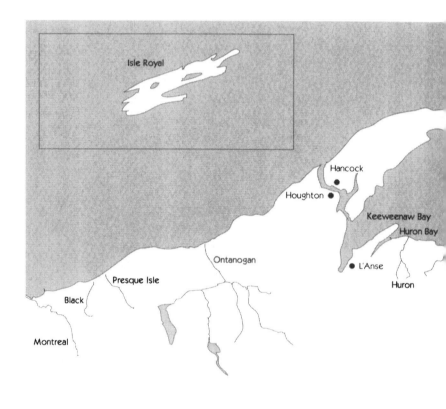

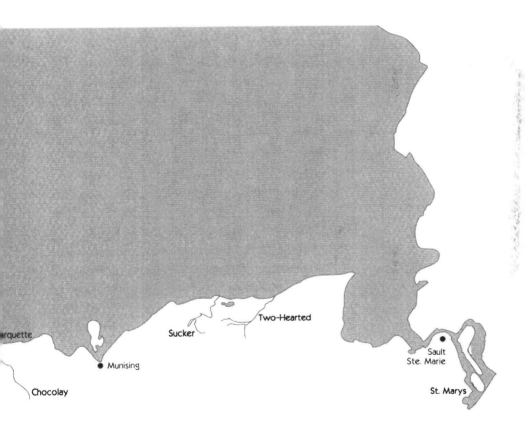

by growing numbers of anglers. No longer will you have the river to yourself. Nevertheless, many miles of water are accessible to steelhead. Of course, many streams in the Upper Peninsula get spring steelhead runs. However, don't expect anyone to tell you about them. Ditto for good places to catch brook trout. Folks in the U.P. know how to keep a secret.

Ontario

Ontario has dozens of streams ranging in size from mighty rivers like the Nipigon and the Pic to tiny creeks. Like Minnesota's streams, they depend on meltwater and runoff for flow, although some rivers, like the Steel, are so large that the best time to fish them is when the water is low. Nearly every river gets a spring steelhead run. Some streams, particularly in the Nipigon area, have remnant coaster brook trout populations. Remember, those few brook trout are more valuable in the lake than they are in the freezer or on the wall. Chinook and coho salmon also run some rivers, especially the big streams. A few, like the Kaministiquia and the Black Sturgeon, have resident populations of walleyes and northern pike. In many instances, a lack of easy access makes Ontario river fishing difficult for all but the most determined anglers.

Starting in the west at Thunder Bay, the Kaministiquia is the first major river. In recent years, the Kam, as it is known, has been heavily stocked with chinook salmon. The river receives a fall salmon run and spring steelhead, but its immense size makes it difficult to fish. Bring a boat or try the tributaries. Smallmouth bass, walleye, and northern pike are caught during the summer. If fishing is slow, visit the "Niagara of the North"—Kakabecka Falls—or the Old Fort William historic fur post, both of which are on the river.

Don't expect anyone to tell you which streams on the U.P. are good for spring steelhead runs. Ditto for good places to catch brook trout. Folks on the U.P. know how to keep a secret.

Thunder Bay steelheaders speak highly of the McIntyre River, which flows through the center of the city. Installation of a fish passageway at a dam in the city allowed the fish access to many miles of upstream spawning water. You can fish the river throughout the city, although the Lakehead University stretch is probably the most popular. Other nearby steelhead streams include the Neebing and McKenzie Rivers. Installation of a fishway at a dam on the Current River may soon add to the stream mileage accessible to Thunder Bay anglers.

The large and lightly fished Wolf and Black Sturgeon Rivers flow into Black Bay. Both have spring and fall runs of steelhead and salmon, although neither river is easy to fish. The Black Sturgeon also has fishable populations of species such as walleye and northern pike.

The mighty Nipigon River is the outlet of Nipigon Lake, which is so large it could almost be considered the sixth Great Lake. Nearly everything swims in the Nipigon, including the huge brook trout for which the river was once famous. However, the construction of three hydroelectric dams along the river flooded the best brook trout habitat and permanently changed the river. You can still catch brook trout weighing up to ten pounds here, but it isn't easy. Expect many hours to pass between strikes, and be prepared for difficult and sometimes dangerous fishing conditions.

East of Nipigon is the scenic Nipigon Bay area, protected by massive St. Ignace Island. A number of smaller streams, such as the Jackpine and Cypress Rivers, enter the bay. Most receive spring steelhead runs. Further east, between Terrace Bay and Marathon, the Steel and Little Pic Rivers pour their substantial flows into Superior. The Steel has spring and fall runs, as well as a resident trout

The mighty Nipigon River is the outlet of Nipigon Lake, which is so large it could almost be considered the sixth Great Lake.

Major Tributaries Along Ontario's Shoreline

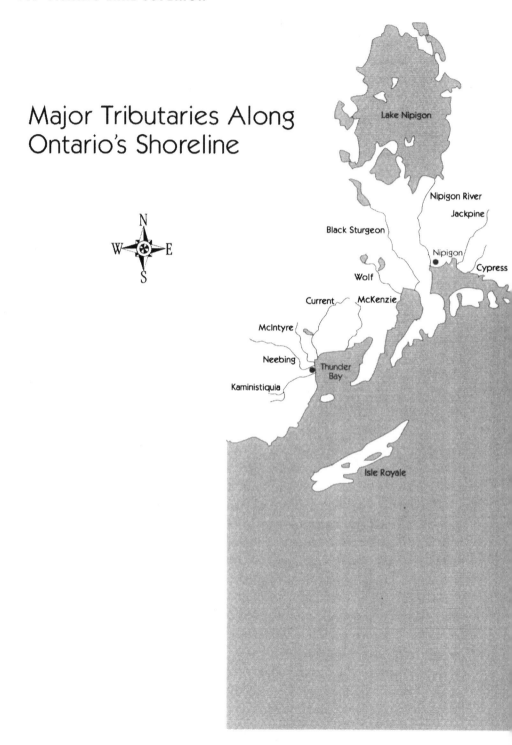

population, but is wide, deep, and fast. Spring floods last into June. Autumn, when water levels are lower, is the best time to fish. The Little Pic is a huge, turbid river that flows through a spectacular canyon. Again, the fishing isn't easy.

From Marathon east to Wawa is the wild Pukaskwa National Park, a wilderness area where the rivers are accessible only by boating or backpacking. Those who have explored the area say the fishing can be fantastic. However, this is not a place for the inexperienced. In spring and fall, be prepared for bouts of winterlike weather. Boaters must negotiate long stretches of exposed shoreline, and return trips can be delayed for days by storms or winds.

At Wawa, the Michipicoten River and its tributary, the Magpie River, flow into Michipicoten Harbor. Upstream fish migrations in the Magpie are blocked by a beautiful waterfall within sight of the Michipicoten. That river, however, offers twelve miles of boatable water up to the dam at Scott Falls. Long known as a premier steelhead stream, the Michipicoten has declined somewhat in recent years. During the 1980s word spread about tremendous runs of huge chinook salmon, which had never been stocked there. Unfortunately, that fishery, too, has fallen off. Nevertheless, it remains one of the finest trout streams flowing into the lake. Other species, such as walleyes, are also caught there.

East of Wawa is the Old Woman River, a beautiful stream where steelhead can travel a fair distance upstream. Expect to have company on the stream. About twenty miles further east is the Agawa River, which is somewhat larger and easier to fish. Flowing into Pancake Bay is the Pancake River, where steelhead and salmon can swim over four miles upstream to Pancake Falls. Fish this one

From Marathon east to Wawa is the wild Pukaskwa National Park, a wilderness area where the rivers are accessible only by boating or backpacking.

before breakfast and you're sure to work up an appetite.

The slow, wide Batchawana River and its tributaries merit some exploration. The river is fairly accessible, and some stretches offer good spring and fall fishing. The nearby Chippewa River is another fine stream, with about two miles of steelhead water. However, those looking to tangle with trophies in *big* water should fish the rapids in the St. Marys River at Sault Ste. Marie. Steelhead and salmon here swim upstream from Lake Huron and are substantially huskier than their Lake Superior brethren. The best fishing spots for drifters are accessible from the Ontario shore.

An Angler's Calendar

FISHING LAKE SUPERIOR successfully depends not only on knowing where and how to catch fish, but knowing where and how to catch fish throughout the year. Weather patterns on the Big Pond shift dramatically over the course of a year, continuously challenging anglers to adjust their methods for success. Below is a calender to help you adapt to Superior's ever-changing weather conditions.

January

The new year usually marks the beginning of the "hardwater" season on Superior, when solid ice begins to form in the large bays. Try shallow-water fishing for splake and brown trout in Chequamegon Bay just after first ice. Look for lake trout farther out. Ice-fishing for lake trout on Thunder Bay starts now, too. In both places, play it safe! Be aware that ice thickness varies. Don't explore new areas unless you are very confident of ice conditions.

This is also when the burbot spawn, migrating upstream beneath the ice of some large rivers. A locally popular winter burbot fishery exists on the Nemadji River in Superior, Wisconsin. In Minnesota, Kamloops rainbows are beginning to

Weather patterns on the Big Pond shift dramatically over the course of a year, continuously challenging anglers to adjust their methods for success.

appear near river mouths. Open water fishing for 'loopers is possible on warm days.

February

If the weather is cold, the open lake starts forming ice during this month. Lake trout "bobbers" venture out from Michigan, Wisconsin, and near Duluth. Be sure you have reliable, up-to-date fishing information before going out, because ice conditions can change daily. In sheltered areas such as Thunder Bay and Chequamegon Bay, adventurous anglers drive out on the ice with four-wheel-drive vehicles. Using a snowmobile or ATV to reach the fishing grounds is a more sensible option. Bobbers who fish the pack ice on the open lake often drag a boat behind them in case winds or currents cause a lead to open in the ice. It is better to leave behind a snowmobile or fishing gear than to be adrift on the ice pack.

March

Elsewhere in the nation, spring is arriving, but on Lake Superior winter drags on. In fact, on cold days the lake is still making ice. Nevertheless, the days get longer and warmer. Fish preparing for the spring spawn become more active and start staging near river mouths. Now is a good time to try fishing for Kamloops rainbows along the Minnesota coast near Duluth and Two Harbors. Deepwater lake trout continue to bite well, too.

Off Superior, Wisconsin, look for walleyes near the Superior Entry, where they stage prior to their spawning run. You can walk out from shore, but be careful. The winds and river currents cause ice conditions to change frequently. Fish for walleyes near the bottom in twenty-five- to fifty-foot depths. Trophies are possible.

April

On the first Saturday of this month, many anglers begin their openwater fishing season with a day on Wisconsin's Bois Brule River. In some years the river is flooded with spring melt, but in others anglers must contend with hip-deep snow. Contending with the conditions is part of the fun, and the reward can be a silvery steelhead. April is the month for steelheaders. Spawning runs in most South Shore streams peak in the middle to latter part of the month. Runs get underway along the Minnesota coast during April, too. In Ontario, however, spring and steelhead won't arrive until May. The smelt run occurs when water temperatures in the streams reach 45 degrees.

Out on the Pond, trollers gear up for coho. Although the fish average less than two pounds in weight, they're tasty. And you can expect fast action. Try Chequamegon Bay shortly after ice-out. Use stick baits on top and troll very slowly.

May

May is an excellent month for trollers, shore-casters, and stream anglers. Chinook salmon, coho, and lakers are active along the South Shore, lake trout congregate near North Shore river mouths, and good numbers of steelhead swim in most streams. Upstream on the tributaries, brook trout are biting. Picking a place to go fishing can be a tough decision.

Trollers can head for South Shore ports such as Duluth, Minnesota; Superior, Port Wing, Cornucopia, Bayfield, Washburn, and Ashland, Wisconsin; and L'Anse, Marquette, and Au Train, Michigan. Small coho salmon, chinooks, and lake trout predominate in the catch. The fish are near the surface, and accessible to small boaters. However, deepwater downrigging for lake trout can be very productive, too.

Shore-casters can work piers, breakwalls, and shoreline areas near Duluth and along the South Shore. On the North Shore, lake temperatures remain very cold, so fish congregate to feed where warm water flows in from the tributaries. Lake trout are the most common catch, with rainbows coming in second. As a rule, you'll find better shore-casting for steelhead off the mouths of Ontario streams. Late spring and early summer provide about the best opportunity for shore-casters to connect with Atlantic salmon along the Minnesota coast.

June

June is the month when summer arrives along the South Shore. Both air and water temperatures warm up, making fishing a more comfortable proposition than it was the month before. Also, the fish are more active. It is not uncommon to fish from the surface to the bottom and find salmon or trout at several depths. On the North Shore, water temps remain cold, although the warmer water gradually starts moving north from Duluth. In Ontario, the protected waters of Thunder Bay and Nipigon Bay start warming up, too.

Coho and chinook salmon congregate along temperature breaks. Salmon schools are migratory, so try to get up-to-date information about where the fishing is hot. One consistent place to try is the mudline off Duluth-Superior. You can also locate salmon along the outer Apostle Islands.

Lake Superior walleyes are also on the prowl. Now is the time to try the St. Louis River estuary, Chequamegon Bay, and Huron Bay. Trolling spinners baited with minnows or worms is a good starting point. In Chequamegon Bay smallmouth bass are becoming active, too. However, remember this is the spawning season. Releasing fat female bass is good conservation.

July

Summer is arriving—slowly—along Minnesota's North Shore. Early in the month expect to find good fishing near Knife River, Two Harbors, and Silver Bay as the cohos and small chinooks begin migrating north. By midmonth you can catch them near Tofte, and then they'll show up at Grand Marais and Hovland. Lake trout will likely out-number salmon in your catch. Much further north, this is a good month to explore the islands off Rossport, Ontario. Along the North Shore, you'll find fish near the top. However, South Shore trollers must go deep or try fishing further off-shore. Smallmouth afficionados should try Batchawana and Chequamegon Bays.

August

This is a month of transition. Early in the month, the only action available at South Shore ports may be deepwater fishing for lake trout. By the end of the month, however, autumn is in the air. Chi-nook salmon stage in the vicinity of river mouths as water temperatures cool down. A few chinooks might ascend the rivers following heavy rains, but the chances of catching them in streams are much better next month.

Now is a good time to try offshore fishing grounds like Isle Royale, Stannard Rock, and the Slate Islands. Travel conditions are generally bet-ter in the first half of the month. Strong autumn breezes start blowing in late August.

September

With September come the chinooks, fat from four years of foraging in the big lake and ready to spawn. Clusters of boats troll off places like Duluth's Lester River, where the huge salmon wait for the autumn rains to raise river levels and trigger their spawning run. In the mighty Nipigon, small boaters troll patiently in the pool below the Alexander Falls dam, which blocks the upstream travels of all fish. And on streams ranging from tiny creeks to roaring rivers, legions of drifters seek to do battle with spawning salmon. Other fish are entering the rivers, too. Fishing is good both in the streams and near the mouths. Coaster brook trout spawn in Ontario tributaries (make sure the fishing season is open and release your catch) and brown trout run along the South Shore.

Lake trout are also starting to move into shoreline areas as they prepare to spawn. Steelhead can be caught in nearshore areas, too. Although trollers have excellent luck in September, prevailing northwest winds can hinder your efforts. Stay flexible and take advantage of nice days. Shore-casters should focus on river mouths and harbor breakwalls.

October

For trollers, October marks the end of the season. In many areas, lake trout seasons close; and other species, such as chinook salmon, are spawning in tributary streams. However, this is a prime month to fish for steelhead in larger rivers like the Chocolay, Bois Brule, Nipigon, and Steel. Steelhead ascend large rivers, winter in deep holes, and then spawn in the early spring. The best fishing usually occurs in the latter half of the month. Be prepared for brutal weather. Because fall steelhead are not in a spawning mode, they are more aggressive than spring-run fish. Spinners and other artificial lures will draw strikes. Streams are generally at lower levels than in the spring, presenting fly-casters with their best opportunities to connect with steelhead.

November

This is the stormiest month on Lake Superior, one best spent sitting on a deer stand. Die-hard steelheaders are still drifting the streams, but the water is cold and the fish lethargic. A late autumn bonus is spawning coho, especially in South Shore streams like the Flag and Cranberry. Shore-casters can look for rainbows near the river mouths. Occasionally, November river fishing for steelhead and salmon is very good, especially if precipitation is followed by warm, stable weather.

December

Intense cold snaps trigger the formation of safe ice on inland lakes and sheltered estuary areas. But Superior doesn't freeze, even when the temperature plunges below zero. Instead the lake broods beneath a shroud of icy mist. Few people fish. However, on Chequamegon Bay hardy anglers go out in small boats and catch splake by vertical jigging. In the shallow bays along the St. Louis River, you can catch crappie and yellow perch through the ice. On warm afternoons, Upper Peninsula drifters look for active steelhead in open holes along the Chocolay River, and a handful of anglers fish for Kamloops rainbows along Minnesota's North Shore. Most anglers, however, contentedly spend their spare time decorating the Christmas tree.

Resources

For further information about fishing, travel, and lodging on and around Lake Superior, contact the following offices:

Minnesota:

Minnesota Travel Information Center / Thompson Hill Office
8525 Skyline Drive
Duluth, MN 55810
(218) 723-4938

Minnesota Department of Natural Resources / Duluth Area Fisheries
5351 North Shore Drive
Duluth, MN 55804
(218) 723-4785

Wisconsin:

Wisconsin Travel Information Center / Superior Office
305 East Second Street
Superior, WI 54880
(715) 392-1662

Wisconsin Department of Natural Resources / Superior Office
1705 Tower Avenue
Superior, WI 54880
(715) 392-7988

Michigan:

Upper Peninsula Travel and Recreational Center
P.O. Box 400
Iron Mountain, MI 49801
(800) 562-7134 (toll free)

Michigan Department of Natural Resources / Recreation Division
P.O. Box 30257
Lansing, MI 48409
(517) 335-4837

Ontario:

North of Superior Tourism Association
1119 East Victoria Avenue
Thunder Bay, OT P7C 1B7
(800) 265-3951 (toll free in North America)

Ontario Ministry of Natural Resources
P.O. Box 5000
Thunder Bay, OT P7C 5G6
(800) 475-1482 (toll free in North America)

Index